Leading through Crisis, Conflict, and Change in Higher Education

Magna Publications
Madison, Wisconsin

Magna Publications
2718 Dryden Drive
Madison, WI 53704
Magnapubs.com

Copyright © 2020 by Magna Publications

The articles in this book have been previously published in *Academic Leader* or have been adapted from a Magna Online Seminar or a Magna 20-Minute Mentor.

ISBN: 978-0-912150-76-5

Compiled by Jon Crylen

All rights reserved. Published 2020. It is unlawful to duplicate, transfer, or transmit this book in any manner without permission from the publisher.

Contents

Introduction 5
Part I: Leading through Crisis 7
   Leading in the Midst of a Crisis 9
   The Need for Multigenerational Workforce Strategies
   during the COVID-19 Crisis 13
   The FOCUS on Faculty Model of Crisis Leadership:
   Remote Leadership across Institutional Contexts 19
   Rethinking Productivity during the COVID-19 Pandemic ... 25
   Crisis Planning Strategies in the #MeToo Era 29
   Supporting the Professional Identities of University Staff
   in Turbulent Times 33
   Survival: The Impetus for Vigorous Undergraduate
   Student Recruitment 37
   Effective Strategies for Increasing Undergraduate
   Student Enrollment 43
   A Challenge to Higher Education Leaders in the
   Wake of a Social Injustice Crisis 49

Part II: Leading through Conflict 53
   Creating Dialogue in the Interest of Social Justice on Campus ... 55
   Campus Civility Project: Emotionally Intelligent Conversations ... 59
   President-Faculty Relations: A Dean's Dilemma? 65
   Managing Conflict: Please Don't Leave 69
   Positive Effects of Conflict 71
   Managing, Not Eliminating, Intradepartmental Conflict 73
   Strategies for Dealing with a Certified Jerk 77
   How to Respond to Toxic Leadership: Six Practical Approaches ... 81
   Developing Critical Cross-cultural Communicative
   Competence in Academic Leaders 85
   Campus Incivility and Free Speech: A Contemporary Dilemma ... 97

Part III: Leading through Change 103
   How to Lead Change from the Middle 105
   Expectation for Continuous Improvement Even during
   Challenging Fiscal Times 111
   Can Innovation Be Taught? 115

Leading Your Academic Department toward Inclusion:
   How to Ensure Faculty Are LGBTQ+
   Competent in the Classroom 119
Laying the Groundwork for Positive, Voluntary
   Technology Changes 123
From Fringe to Mainstream: Increasing the Acceptance of
Online Education on Your Campus... 129
Five Strategies to Improve the Quality of Online Education
on Your Campus 133
Accessibility: Making a Plan to Do What's Right (and Required) 137
How to Encourage Faculty to Adopt OER 143
Both Sides Now: Creating a Culture of UDL 147
Program Acquisitions: Lessons for Leaders.. 151

About the Contributors **155**
Additional Resources **162**

Introduction

It's no secret that US higher education is in crisis.

The reasons are well-known. Demographic shifts portend a future of declining enrollment. State appropriations for public colleges and universities continue to dwindle, forcing schools to cut expenses and rely ever more on nonresidential tuition payments. The enormous financial burden of attending college (outstanding student loan debt totals nearly $1.6 trillion) has students and their parents questioning the value of a four-year degree. And now, of course, there's the unchecked pandemic, which has forced higher education leaders into decisions they never counted on having to make—from overseeing rapid online course migration to shuttering programs and laying off tenured faculty—and figures to change a great deal about how colleges and universities operate.

While it may be tempting to regard higher ed more or less hyperbolically as defined by a set of converging catastrophes, academic life nonetheless remains colored by more familiar, relatively mundane challenges, including managing intradepartmental conflict, maintaining trust between faculty and administration, and upholding institutional commitments to diversity, equity, and inclusion. Such issues will continue to confront chairs, deans, and other academic leaders even as weathering the fallout from the pandemic commands the bulk of their attention.

As they face quandaries of varying scale and complexity and seek to transform their departments, schools, and institutions, academic leaders need guidance. This book provides it, and the contents break down into three parts. Part one, "Leading through Crisis," is the most topical; it addresses not only pandemic response but also strategies for dealing with undergraduate recruitment amid shrinking enrollments, sexual harassment and assault allegations against faculty and staff, and systemic racial injustice as it bears on student life. Part two, "Leading through Conflict," turns to more enduring issues, including civility and social justice on campus, free speech issues, and ways to handle discordant and toxic relations within and across campus units. Finally, part three, "Leading through Change," offers pointers on less heated challenges, such as improving online education, making technology changes, meeting accessibility requirements, adopting open educational resources, and embracing the principles of universal design for learning.

The articles in this book are meant to stand alone, so feel free to jump around as you read. Some pieces make natural pairings with one another, but none provides a guiding idea essential to the any other. What the different pieces share is an emphasis on practical, actionable advice provided by and for academic leaders. Regardless of your leadership role, I hope you come away from this book with ideas and strategies that help you better manage crises, resolve conflict, and spearhead change on your campus.

—*Jon Crylen*

PART 1
Leading Through Crisis

Leading in the Midst of a Crisis

Tanjula Petty

We have all heard the cliché that just as the sun shines, it will surely rain. I am even guilty of saying there are no two days alike in my world as each day brings a unique experience or challenge to be resolved. I believe I speak for all higher education administrators in saying that while we have had some difficult days, none compare to those we have recently faced as relates to the COVID-19 pandemic and preparing our campuses to be responsive. Sadly, this is not the first time some of us have had to ready our campuses for emergencies. As I reflect, it was only three years ago—while I was serving as the vice president of academic affairs at Albany Technical College in Albany, Georgia—that the community was hit by two massive tornadoes within the span of 10 days. This devastating event entailed the destruction of homes, damaged the technological infrastructure of the campus, and resulted in many fatalities.

On account of this past experience, I believe I was more able to use emotional intelligence in making sure that my current institution, Alabama State University, covered all its bases as we approached the COVID-19 crisis. Emotional intelligence is essential for higher educational administrators to effectively balance the multiple challenges of leading various initiatives, including unexpected emergencies. Emotionally intelligent administrators are able to connect with stakeholders in ways that produce efficient and effective results to continuously carryout missions and visions. Below are some emotionally intelligent strategies to help higher education leaders be proactive rather than reactive as they face the current crisis.

Prioritize the health, safety, and well-being of your faculty, staff, and students

Safety on campus is a primary concern and is a joint responsibility of administrators, faculty, staff, and students. At the forefront of your conversations with your leadership teams must be how you must protect your staff, students, your organization, and potentially the public as we are dealing with "social distancing." It does not matter what decision you make; there will be some backlash. But there are no two institutions that will handle this situation the same. You must make the best decision for your institution. In the age of social media, students will take to the internet to vent their frustrations, and when faculty disagree with your decision, you can expect many emails about their perceptions. Once you make a decision, however, stand by it and do not waiver, especially if you know what is in the best interest of all involved. I always ask this question in a crisis: Are my decisions ethical, legal, and moral? Are they in the best interests of faculty, staff, students, and the public? If you can answer yes to those questions, you have made the right decisions for your respective institution.

Engage and involve all players

Make sure all the right team players are at the table and represent every critical area of your institution. As your leadership team meets, it is important to have academic and student affairs present as instruction and student activities may be impeded. For example, at Albany Technical College, we delayed instruction for four weeks after the tornadoes, which meant ensuring faculty were prepared to restructure course curriculum to meet the challenges we faced. Student activities were delayed and had to be rescheduled. In the case of COVID-19, like many institutions we have allowed students to return home, in turn having to transition over 1,700 face-to-face courses into the online format. As relates to the students, especially the class of 2020, we find ourselves canceling and postponing commencement ceremonies. Additionally, communications or public affairs must be present to ensure that the messaging your campus rolls out is consistent. Importantly, facilities, public safety, operations, and technology personnel must be present to offer feedback from their respective areas. It is at this time that you must explicitly spell out goals so that everyone has the same agenda and can achieve optimum outcomes for the institution. Everyone's safety should be on the agenda and a priority action item.

Follow your EOP

Your institution should have an emergency operations plan (EOP) that outlines how it will respond to emergencies such as pandemics. Ensure that your staff has annual training and possible situational training on the procedures in this document. The one thing I have been most appreciative of at my prior and current institutions has been the annual training done to help prepare the campus for the "just in case." Well, the "just in case" is upon us, and we must be responsive. Importantly, appoint someone to maintain, oversee, and be responsible for updating the EOP as well as oversee emergency readiness on campus. The EOP should guide your actions in all scenarios.

Be prepared to execute

If you are like me, you've been lucky never to receive a crisis alert before arriving at the office in the morning. Events just happen, however, and you will need to be prepared to execute what is outlined in your EOP. Everyone will be caught off guard, and to be approaching or in the midst of a crisis is not the time to have long meetings or conversations about what will and will not work. Now is the time for calm and direct leadership. Managing the crisis will require planned responses, efficient communications, and effective execution. There is no doubt you will have to think fast on your feet, work smart, and make informed, data-driven decisions now and in the future.

Provide consistent communication

As a leader in higher education, one of the most important skills you can have is the ability to effectively communicate. I have always been one to get in front of a story by preparing detailed and transparent communications acknowledging the crisis situation. Prepare a communication plan that will speak to all stakeholders. One of the initial tasks should be identifying the internal and external stakeholders who matter to your institution. You will possibly need multiple communications for faculty, staff, students, and external stakeholders. Although you are in a critical situation, do not feel pressured to give a premature statement, as it is not advised that you react without adequate information. Make sure that your team is providing the right type of information so you can proceed with determining the appropriate response. Make sure that your communication is consistent, responsive, and transparent. Also make sure that you are sharing the communication through various mediums. Currently, my institution has developed a host website for COVID-19, but we share the information via email and social media to reach as many stakeholders as possible.

Calculate the costs

There are financial costs associated with operating in crisis mode. Therefore, you must monitor the cost of institutional needs to ensure that operations continue. For example, in the COVID-19 pandemic many institutions are finding themselves transitioning instruction and student services online. Institutions are finding creative ways to implement new technologies and provide training to their respective campus communities. There is a price tag attached to such training and new technologies. Additionally, keeping your faculty engaged and prepared to teach effectively online will have a price as well. Additionally, as federal and state agencies reach out to institutions, you will want to be prepared to provide an estimated cost if your institutional is eligible for emergency grants or loans.

I have often heard the quote, "A person's true character is often revealed in time of crisis or temptation. Make sure that you have what it takes to be your best in such times" (Dr. Paul T. P. Wong). Knowing how you will operate during a crisis is one of the most critical lessons a leader can learn. I refer back to the introduction: having emotional intelligence and leading with a calmness will be to your advantage. If you have a leadership role in higher education, there are opportunities that can help you prepare to operate in a crisis situation. Importantly, I have learned to find opportunity in calamity, and I have gained resilience and a vision that sees no barriers. I am committed throughout this crisis to ensuring my institution comes out of it stronger than ever and to remaining ready to serve the needs of our students and community.

The Need for Multigenerational Workforce Strategies during the COVID-19 Crisis

Edna B. Chun and Alvin Evans

Higher education leaders tasked with determining whether to reopen campuses in fall 2020 or spring 2021 face a myriad of challenges. With dramatic budget reductions, decreased tuition revenues, reduced state support, and declining enrollment, a shock wave of staff layoffs and furloughs has ensued. Decisions are being made about closing academic programs and departments and potentially even terminating tenured faculty. For example, Ohio University announced three successive rounds of budget cuts that resulted in the layoff of 53 non-tenure-track positions and elimination of 94 administrator positions, 140 unionized positions in dining and maintenance, and 81 other classified and administrative positions. In another example, the University of Alaska Board of Regents voted to reduce or eliminate more than 40 academic programs, including undergraduate majors in sociology, chemistry and earth science as well as graduate programs in English, biochemistry, and management information systems.

As the coronavirus-induced crisis deepens, the question arises as to the role ageism will play in employment decisions relating to the administrative, faculty, and staff workforce and in the kinds of measures campuses will implement to facilitate partial or full reopening. A *Los Angeles Times* article (Newberry, 2020) warns in its headline, "The pandemic has amplified ageism. 'It's open season for discrimination' against older adults."

Surprisingly, a number of statements issued by prominent university presidents appear to ignore the concerns of faculty and the risks they may encounter as campuses reopen as well as the potential for transmission of

COVID-19 in multiple college settings. These announcements fail to consider the fact that half of faculty are over 35, and 17 percent are older than 65 (Finkelstein et al., 2016). The age profile of staff is similar, with the average age being 45. And according to federal data, the number of adult learners has increased, with 7.4 million over age 25 now enrolled in college.

Furthermore, the effects of ageism are not limited to older adults but involve both ends of the age spectrum. Although the coronavirus does pose greater risks for older individuals, it also affects younger persons and individuals of all ages with serious underlying medical conditions. A March 16, 2020, analysis by the Centers for Disease Control and Prevention found that 38 percent of hospitalizations were for individuals between ages 20 and 54. with half of those in intensive care being younger than 65 (Maragakis, 2020). In addition, a recent article by eight psychologists warns against the use of arbitrary age cutoffs and points out the negative effects of stress and loneliness on younger individuals (Ayalon et al., 2020). Importantly, the researchers emphasize the need for intergenerational solidarity rather than intergenerational division, especially when resources are scarce.

With these pressing concerns in mind, how can campus leadership capitalize on intergenerational synergy? How can policy decisions and public statements reinforce the need for intergenerational solidarity and avoid ageism in employment and downsizing processes?

In our forthcoming book, *Leveraging Multigenerational Workforce Strategies in Higher Education*, we draw from in-depth interviews and research findings to argue that intergenerational capabilities are a competitive force that differentiates institutional performance, enhances creativity, and promotes knowledge transfer and problem-solving. Take a study of 18,000 firms in Germany, which found that a 10 percent increase in age diversity resulted in a 3.5 percent annual increase in productivity, as measured in sales, due to diverse problem-solving capabilities. These capabilities arose from different knowledge pools and the transfer of know-how and norms from older to younger cohorts (Backes-Gellner et al., 2011). Similarly, on the academic side, consider the advantages of multigenerational collaboration shared by Chris Keys, a retired psychology professor from DePaul University: "If you have a critical mass of good people at each level, and . . . they appreciate each other and their contributions, then you really have the ingredients of a positive, multigenerational department."

We also document the ways that ageist framing in the academic workplace can have long-term effects on faculty, administrators and staff at both ends of the age spectrum. Administrators, staff, and even tenured faculty can experience pressure to retire or retire early. Younger tenure-stream faculty too can face significant hurdles in the promotion and tenure process based on normative views of career progression. Administrators and contingent faculty have few due process protections and can be subject to ageist framing in employment processes. A central finding of our study is that ageist pressures are magnified and intensified due to the intersectionality of race and ethnicity, gender, and sexual orientation.

Consider, for example, the ordeal faced by Susan, a white female tenured professor, who endured the overt discriminatory actions of her white male chair designed to force her to retire. He loaded her schedule with undergraduate required courses and excluded her from the graduate course rotation for five years. He then accused her of refusing to work with graduate students. To try to catch her making any inadvertent remarks to students that he could use against her, the chair embarked on a surveillance campaign by pacing in front of her office during office hours:

> He would pace in the hall and listen to everything I said to the students. So I was under constant visual and audio surveillance by him every time I had office hours. . . . He had a lot of hours to pace in the hall in front of my office and try to catch me doing something illegal, which he never did. . . . I had to experience that for a long time, the constant pacing in front of my office. It was incredibly stressful.

It was only when Susan began the process of filing a formal complaint of ageism and the chair left the department that the harassment stopped. As Susan concludes, "A lot of it was ageism, He wanted to have the only authority and he didn't want to have any counter forces. He didn't want to have different perspectives."

Given the potential for increased ageism in institutional processes driven by resource scarcity, we offer for consideration several leadership strategies that will help build workforce synergy and ensure intergenerational collaboration:

1. **Consult with campus constituencies and include different generational perspectives in the university or college decision-making processes, such as in the development of restructuring, downsizing, and reopening strategies.** A major complaint that has arisen on a number of campuses is that university or college administration is not consulting actively with campus governance and faculty, administrators, and staff in decisions affecting their future. These decisions can range from the shrinking of academic programs to determining the readiness and safety of reopening. Since individuals may risk their health to maintain their positions, active dialogue and

consultation is needed to develop appropriate strategies and temporary workforce alternatives.

2. **Incorporate checks and balances on decision-making to ensure intergenerational equity.** Close monitoring of employment processes—including layoffs, furloughs, and program and departmental closures—is essential to prevent differential treatment based on age and other protected characteristics. Engage human resource and diversity officers in conducting systematic workforce analyses that maintain intergenerational equity and address the potential for ageism in organizational outcomes.

3. **Ensure that public statements reflect the needs and concerns of all campus constituencies and reflect an appreciation for the contributions of intergenerational talent.** Addressing the concerns of faculty, staff, and administrators in campus statements is critical. For example, in a widely critiqued op-ed, Brown University president Christina Paxson (2020) argued for reopening Ivy League institutions but mentioned only the loss of revenue rather than the dangers to faculty and staff. As she stated, "The basic business model for most colleges and universities is simple—tuition comes twice a year at the beginning of each semester. . . . Remaining closed in the fall means losing as much as half of our revenue."

4. **Develop a strategic, institutional approach to voluntary separation and phased retirement programs.** Many institutions have implemented voluntary separation plans that allow eligible faculty, administrators, and staff to leave the institution on their own timetable and receive a monetary incentive. These plans offer employees choice in their future plans while permitting colleges and universities to address budgetary shortfalls and align vacant positions with current academic priorities. Similarly, phased and deferred retirement programs permit the continued contributions of senior faculty and staff and ensure a smooth transition process to retirement.

With the difficult process ahead of determining when to reopen and how to address significant budgetary shortfalls, it has become even more important for institutions of higher education to evaluate the impact of decisions on different generational cohorts. The vitality, creativity, knowledge, and know-how of a multigenerational workforce are critical assets that will help institutions cope with the COVID-19 crisis and sustain their academic mission of student learning and success.

References

Ayalon, L., Chasteen, A., Diehl, M., Levy, B. R., Neupert, S. D., Rothermund, K., Tesch-Römer, C., & Wahl, H.-W. (2020). Aging in times of the COVID-19 pandemic: Avoiding ageism and fostering intergenerational solidarity. *The Journals of Gerontology: Series B*. Advance online publication. https://doi.org/10.1093/geronb/gbaa051

Backes-Gellner, U., Schneider, M. R., & Veen, S. (2011). Effect of workforce age on quantitative and qualitative organizational performance: Conceptual framework and case study evidence. *Organization Studies, 32*(8), 1103–1121. https://doi.org/10.1177/0170840611416746

Finkelstein, M. J., Conley, V. M., & Schuster, J. H. (2016). *The faculty factor: Reassessing the American academy in a turbulent era.* Johns Hopkins University Press.

Maragakis, L. L. (2020, April 9). *Coronavirus and COVID-19: Younger adults are at risk, too.* https://www.hopkinsmedicine.org/health/conditions-and-diseases/coronavirus/coronavirus-and-covid-19-younger-adults-are-at-risk-too

Newberry, L. (2020, May 1). The pandemic has amplified ageism. "It's open season for discrimination" against older adults. *Los Angeles Times.* https://www.latimes.com/california/story/2020-05-01/coronavirus-pandemic-has-amplified-ageism

Paxson, C. (2020, April 26). College campuses must reopen in the fall. Here's how we do it. *The New York Times.* https://www.nytimes.com/2020/04/26/opinion/coronavirus-colleges-universities.html

The FOCUS on Faculty Model of Crisis Leadership: Remote Leadership Support across Institutional Contexts

Russell Carpenter, Michael G. Strawser, Kevin Dvorak, Timothy Forde, and Masha Krsmanovic

Articles lamenting the post-COVID-19 state of higher education have reached their zenith (we hope!). But after countless explorations of this pandemic's effects on the state of enrollment (Hartocollis, 2020), study abroad opportunities and tuition revenue (Whalen, 2020), job placement and course modalities (Gardner, 2020), and, of course, overall budgets (Huelsman, 2020), few have positioned COVID-19 as an opportunity for faculty development professionals to respond urgently to faculty needs in an effort to support and enhance student learning. To address this concern, we developed an actionable and transferable model to help institutional leaders FOCUS on faculty in times of crisis.

FOCUS provides a model for faculty leadership that transcends operational and institutional contexts, especially amid challenges. The model consists of five elements for effectively leading faculty, with a focus on times of remote instruction. Many available leadership models require time-consuming, costly, and intensive training, often involving travel to a specific site or conference. Many academic leaders have been left on their own, however, as entire institutions have quickly moved instruction, operations, and administration to remote delivery, thus creating challenges with traditional leadership training opportunities. We need, then, portable, accessible leadership models that transcend academic disciplines and institutional contexts.

FOCUS emphasizes timely, faculty-centered leadership. It can be used as a scaffolded, five-step process or adapted for institutional leadership contexts or challenges (figure 1).

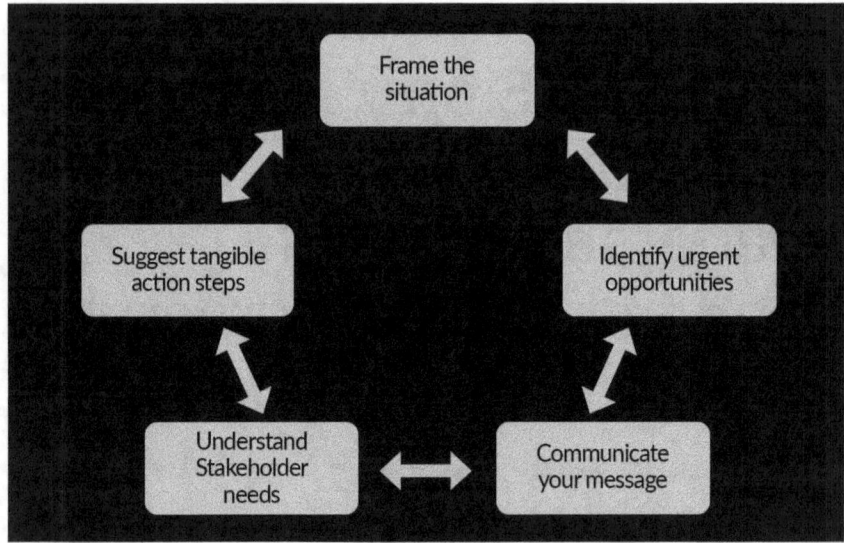

Figure 1. The FOCUS model of leadership

1. Frame the situation

Frame the situation by first defining it and identifying how academic leaders—alongside their faculty—should develop a plan for moving forward. In the process, consider the level of transparency needed to engage faculty stakeholders. While all information—including data, input, or feedback—may not be known at this time, it is still important to be honest and straightforward in times of crisis. But leaders should be appropriately transparent without causing information overload or an infodemic. To do this, focus on the facts of the situation rather than your own inferences and frame the situation as accurately as possible.

1. What is the current impact on teaching and learning, student success, and faculty engagement?
2. What are the potential short- and long-term impacts on teaching and learning, student success, and faculty engagement?
3. In what ways might this situation affect faculty (e.g., in terms of tenure, teaching, or research)?

2. Identify urgent opportunities

After framing the situation, identify urgent opportunities—that is, the circumstances, contexts, or situations that require immediate attention. As you do so, consider approaches, possibilities, or alternatives for operationalizing activity using familiar and new technologies or software to best engage faculty. The process might involve assessing areas under your purview that are most at risk or could benefit and, specific to faculty development, where your leadership efforts most affect faculty.

1. How might you leverage available funds or institutional support to best implement technologies and media?
2. How might you seek external support to implement new technologies? Are there possibilities to partner with external groups that share similar goals?
3. How might you reconsider current practices to improve efficiency?

3. Communicate your message

After framing the situation and identifying urgent opportunities, start to select the most appropriate channels for communicating your message. Try not to overwhelm and instead think strategically about how faculty consume information most efficiently and effectively. The answers to the questions below will probably depend on your faculty, the institution, and the ethos of information seekers.

1. Timing and frequency: How often will faculty benefit from your communication? What is appropriate for the moment? Is it daily, a few times a week, once a week?
2. What is the best medium to deliver each message? Is it email? A virtual meeting platform, such as Zoom or GoToMeeting? Group text messaging?
3. Should the message be delivered in a way that invites interaction (e.g., via a listserv or virtual meeting platform), or should it be delivered in a way that is static (e.g., a webpage update)?

4. Understand stakeholder needs

Throughout the process, ensure that needs are understood in your area. Ask colleagues about their concerns rather than make assumptions. Try to identify what faculty need to continue to do their jobs effectively.

1. Ask faculty how they are handling the crisis and what they need to be successful throughout the situation.
2. Assess what it will take (e.g., funding, resources, or collaboration) to ensure that faculty needs are met.

3. Give faculty opportunities to provide regular feedback on the extent to which their needs have been met.

5. **S**uggest tangible action steps

Finally, think deeply about these questions and communicate appropriately while considering tangible action steps that need to be taken immediately to succeed, and then establish frameworks to complete the action steps. Make sure expectations, suggestions, and recommendations are clear, concise, and actionable.

1. What steps should be taken to ensure that student learning continues at a high level?
2. How do faculty need to be supported in taking care of themselves, their families, or other personal or professional obligations?
3. Determine tangible and appropriate ways to continue supporting faculty (e.g., with promotion or tenure applications or committee work) using available resources.

By implementing the FOCUS model, leaders can situate faculty development as a robust institutional resource in trying times. Remember to frame the situation, identify urgent opportunities, communicate your message, understand stakeholder needs, and suggest tangible action steps.

While this concept of leadership amid remote delivery of institutional programs and courses might differ from traditionally defined leadership, several considerations rise to the top: the need for timely information among a variety of priorities for quality and accessibility. The FOCUS leadership model suggests an attention to concerns raised by faculty and for the welfare of faculty and their students. Several possible paths for implementing FOCUS emerge as well, including

- trying one area of the model based on concerns, changes, challenges, opportunities, or needs of your faculty, department, college, or campus;
- inviting discussion about the FOCUS model among your colleagues;
- adding to the FOCUS model in ways that support your immediate and long-term needs and goals; and
- welcoming feedback on your implementation or interpretation of the FOCUS model.

It is often tempting to simply survive the moment instead of considering how the current crisis makes faculty development indispensable. Now, maybe more than ever, faculty need support to teach online, deliver course material and collaborate with a range of institutional stakeholders in a virtual context, and take care of their families at home. Who better than faculty development professionals to lead this digital army into the next phase and truly FOCUS on faculty?

References

Carpenter, R., Strawser, M. G., Dvorak, K., Forde, T., & Krsmanovic, M. (2020). The implications of COVID-19 on educators, students, curricula, and faculty development. *Journal of Faculty Development, 34*(2), 9–14.

Gardner, L. (2020, March 20). Covid-19 has forced higher ed to pivot to online learning. Here are 7 takeaways so far. *The Chronicle of Higher Education.* https://www.chronicle.com/article/Covid-19-Has-Forced-Higher-Ed/248297

Hartocollis, A. (2020, April 15). After coronavirus, colleges worry: Will students come back? *The New York Times.* https://www.nytimes.com/2020/04/15/us/coronavirus-colleges-universities-admissions.html

Huelsman, M. (2020, March 12). Coronavirus could cause long-term higher ed crisis. *Inside Higher Ed.* https://www.insidehighered.com/views/2020/03/12/coronavirus-could-have-long-term-impact-state-funding-universities-opinion

Whalen, B. (2020, April 14). Education abroad in a post-COVID-19 world. *Inside Higher Ed.* https://www.insidehighered.com/views/2020/04/14/how-covid-19-will-change-education-abroad-american-students-opinion

Rethinking Productivity during the COVID-19 Pandemic

Marissa Greenberg and Elizabeth Williamson

Despite the unprecedented impact of COVID-19 on higher education, recent discussions of productivity have been surprisingly traditional. *Productivity* continues to mean scholarly output in the form of monographs, peer-reviewed articles, conferences presentations, and grant proposals in a particular field of academic study.

This definition of productivity holds regardless of advice about how best to achieve it. Some academics advise embracing physical distancing as an opportunity for a kind of scholarly retreat. Many more urge letting go of writing for the time being and focusing on physical and mental health. Why? Because self-care now will reap scholarly rewards in the future (Ahmad, 2020).

This advice has been adopted, to some degree, by administrators at colleges and universities who are pushing through extensions to tenure clocks, recognizing that the pandemic is interfering with the scholarly output of faculty at every rank. The crisis has also curtailed the process of reviewing grant and article submissions, book manuscripts, and tenure and promotion files, thus slowing the progress of productivity's conventional documentation for everyone while exacerbating practices that exclude women and people of color (Flaherty, 2020; Pettit, 2020).

Kicking the can down the road is necessary right now, but it is not a long-term solution. On the contrary, upheavals to our regular rhythms provide opportunities to combat the long-standing inequities that the crisis has brought into sharp relief and must prompt us to rethink our shared definition of productivity.

Teaching

Whether administrations favor synchronous meeting applications or asynchronous learning management systems, the move to online teaching has meant that faculty have had to acquire new proficiencies, both technical and pedagogical, at a speed often unseen in higher education.

Faculty who previously relied on charisma and expertise to engage students and fill contact hours must now be more strategic about instructional design and make difficult decisions about content delivery and assessment mechanisms, especially given the significant distractions students are facing in their personal lives (Brown & Mangan, 2020).

As we continue to restructure fall classes, some instructors are shifting away from entrenched models of disciplinary mastery and toward innovative models that embrace a variety of competencies, allowing us to teach to students' unique needs and goals. Many institutions have begun to move in this direction by dedicating resources to faculty training in accessible media, authentic assessments, and creative and collaborative projects.

This moment of widespread engagement invites us to devise new mechanisms for documenting productive academic labor. For example, rather than throwing out student evaluations written during COVID-19 (American Association of University Professors, n.d.; Modern Language Association Executive Council 2020), faculty might use this feedback as a baseline against which to demonstrate effort and evolution in teaching. For their part, programs and departments might recruit external reviewers to contribute teaching expertise to a review of tenure and promotion files. By truly weighing teaching equally with scholarship, we begin to acknowledge pedagogy as productivity.

Care work

COVID-19 is also encouraging faculty to embrace new forms of student support. Our colleagues in K–12 have long been more attentive to their role in facilitating all aspects of student development, and the renewed national focus on their skill and resilience should spur tenured and tenure-track faculty to recognize that care work is essential to their more privileged positions as well.

As colleges and universities serve increasingly diverse student populations, it becomes harder and harder to deny that faculty are being called upon, whether implicitly or explicitly, to do care work. The urgency of our students' needs is compounded by crises that threaten to become more frequent—not just the current pandemic and its long-term impacts on students' well-being, but also global trends like climate change.

Working under crisis conditions is a familiar scenario for many of our colleagues. Faculty who occupy one or more marginalized identity positions have long done more than their fair share of peer and student mentorship and diversity and inclusion work (Flaherty, 2019). Yet a robust record of such service remains less likely to secure retention or promotion than a solid list of publications.

To address the imbalance between what students need and what the profession rewards, we must take a hard look at how historically underrepresented faculty have created the conditions for the rest of us to perform conventional forms of productivity. Like ensuring that children eat breakfast before going to school, this highly gendered, classed, and racialized work is necessary, not ancillary, to the more visible work of producing scholarship.

Once we acknowledge this reality, we can consider what it means to fairly compensate faculty who have experience performing care work while navigating traditional academic structures. And we must design meaningful training and support structures for faculty who need them. These changes go beyond renegotiating tenure clocks (American Association of University Professors, n.d.), moving us instead toward a new landscape in which care work is fully valued.

Faculty development

We all benefit from the crowdsourcing of proficiencies generated by the goodwill of our fellow faculty. So it is refreshing to see these existing skill sets garnering the attention that they deserve. From creators on social media to centers for teaching and learning at individual institutions to the education industrial complex, leaders in higher education are spotlighting best practices from around the globe.

This kind of faculty development, like teaching and care work, has been traditionally excluded from definitions of productivity. Peer teaching and learning is invisible labor until a faculty member chooses not to participate and risks losing the designation of "team player." At the same time, faculty who choose to participate may be uneasy or uncertain about how to document this challenging work.

Professional organizations and academic institutions can take a leading role in changing these conditions. For instance, they might establish programs that support sustained collaboration and mentorship, or advocate for hiring, retention, and promotion practices that give weight to public-facing engagement.

The current global health crisis is shining a light on productivity that has always been crucial to facilitating student learning, and our focus on this important work need not end when we return to something resembling normality. In this extraordinary moment, academic leaders have the opportunity to shift their thinking as well as their policies and practices. They have the chance to create a professional environment in which this kind of labor is openly acknowledged as productive, thereby contributing to the broader process of reimagining the social function of higher education.

References

Ahmad, A. S. (2020, March 27). Why you should ignore all that coronavirus-inspired productivity pressure. *The Chronicle of Higher Education*. https://www.chronicle.com/article/Why-You-Should-Ignore-All-That/248366

American Association of University Professors. (n.d.). *AAUP principles and standards for the COVID-19 crisis*. https://www.aaup.org/aaup-principles-and-standards-covid-19-crisis

Brown, S., & Mangan, K. (2020, May 28). What college students need now. *The Chronicle of Higher Education*. https://www.chronicle.com/article/What-College-Students-Need-Now/248882

Flaherty, C. (2019, June 4). Undue burden. *Inside Higher Ed*. https://www.insidehighered.com/news/2019/06/04/whos-doing-heavy-lifting-terms-diversity-and-inclusion-work

Flaherty, C. (2020, April 21). No room of one's own. *Inside Higher Ed*. https://www.insidehighered.com/news/2020/04/21/early-journal-submission-data-suggest-covid-19-tanking-womens-research-productivity

Modern Language Association Executive Council. (2020, March). *Statement on COVID-19 and academic labor*. https://www.mla.org/About-Us/Governance/Executive-Council/Executive-Council-Actions/2020/Statement-on-COVID-19-and-Academic-Labor

Pettit, E. (2020, May 26). Being a woman in academe has its challenges. A global pandemic? Not helping. *The Chronicle of Higher Education*. https://www.chronicle.com/article/Being-a-Woman-in-Academe-Has/248852

Crisis Planning Strategies in the #MeToo Era

Eden Gillott Bowe

The #MeToo movement raised awareness as to the prevalence of sexual assault and sexual harassment in business, politics, and academia. Consider a few of the recent high-profile cases involving universities:

- In March 2018, Michigan State University's dean of osteopathic medicine was arrested and charged with mishandling abuse complaints against Larry Nasser, and two months later MSU agreed to pay $500 million to victims.
- In May 2018, USC's president was forced out over his handling of several scandals, including misconduct toward female students.
- In August 2018, the *New York Times* reported about a respected female NYU professor accused of verbally and physically harassing a male PhD student.

Let's look at what you need to know *now* so you can effectively handle problems in the future that will affect your university's reputation.

Protect yourself by being proactive

If you've ever ridden the subway in New York City, you know the rule "If you see something, say something." Never ignore, cover up, or take steps that make it appear you're covering up a situation.

As soon as you become aware of a complaint, investigate it. Don't brush it aside, or you may create a crisis that could have been avoided.

If there are multiple complaints against a "star" faculty member or an administrator who brings in lots of grants or donations, it may be tempting to look the other way. Don't do it. Even though it may seem like a difficult decision at the time, the safety of your students and the reputation of your university are at stake.

Be careful what you put into writing. This is important on two levels. It's critical to avoid legal trouble, and you should never commit jokes or inappropriate comments to writing. They will come back to haunt you, and the public will tear you apart. Better yet, remove inappropriate comments from your thoughts and conversations entirely.

Handling legal issues
Regardless of whether the situation begins with a lawsuit, make sure legal affairs is brought in early and consulted often. Their purpose is to protect you and the university. They can't do their job effectively if you don't involve them.

When should you go public?
The same is true with public relations. When to go public and what to say (and not say) are strategic. But one rule is basic: the sooner the better. If the issue is likely to become public, you want to be the one who discloses it.

Why? This gives you more control over the conversation. Whoever goes first sets the tone of the story. While you don't want to rush out armed with misinformation, you must avoid looking like you waited until you were forced to disclose.

Conversely, if you are aware of an issue and sit on that information for months (or years), the public blowback will be fierce. You will destroy your credibility. And once trust is lost, it's hard to regain.

What about staff, donors, and other stakeholders? In addition to the media, you need to communicate with your various stakeholders. While each group will have different concerns and questions, your underlying message to all of them needs to be the same. Remember that anything you say to one group may be heard by others and anything you send to anyone may get leaked to the media.

Who should be the spokesperson?
It depends on who's qualified and credible and who's comfortable speaking on the university's behalf. The dean, head of the department in question, or director of communications are usually the face of the organization.

Make sure you or your spokesperson is prepared with talking points that have been carefully crafted, scrubbed of any PR no-nos, and approved by general counsel. Stick to the talking points, and don't go off-script. If it's an extremely sensitive or high-stakes legal issue, your attorney may be the best to insulate you from saying something that may get you into hot water legally.

What should be said and what shouldn't?

It's a delicate balance that depends on the specific situation and the university's values. Choose your words carefully.

Never lie because the truth always seems to find a way into the light.

Never speculate because there may be inaccurate information. Speculation can inadvertently feed into people's fears and open you up to legal trouble.

Be sympathetic but not overly emotional. Talk about what you're doing to fix the issue and make sure it never happens again. Address the issue without minimizing its importance but focus on the future.

Don't use emotionally charged words, even if the media is using them. Never say, "No comment." That makes you look guilty.

Can you just hide from reporters?

No. Make sure that all staff understand the importance of having a designated spokesperson who's responsible for delivering accurate information. Your staff should be trained to say with confidence, "The best person for you to speak to on this matter is [name of spokesperson], our [title]."

How to handle unsubstantiated allegations

Extremely carefully. Treat each complaint seriously. If your investigation finds the allegation(s) to be unsubstantiated, consult with legal affairs, have the appropriate official respond with the investigator's conclusions, and offer an opportunity for the accuser to provide more information (if available).

The when, how, and if of conducting an investigation

While you should do an internal investigation, you also often want to hire an independent investigator. This sends the message that you've got nothing to hide and are committed to learning the truth.

Conversely, the optics can be bad if you rely solely on an internal investigation and it finds no fault. Even if it finds a few issues, the public may believe the most damning "facts" are being swept under the rug.

Justifying termination or discipline

You're never going to make everyone happy. Some people will always think you should have done more. Others will believe you overreacted.

Which is the best route? Consult with your legal department or counsel. Keep public communications brief and succinct.

Moving forward

Live up to your promises. Tighten your processes. Make sure that the university's culture is aligned and adopts the changes. Actions speak louder than words. People have an incredible capacity to forgive. But don't abuse it—or the public's reaction may be fierce.

Editor's note: The focus of this article is on communication advice and not responsible employee procedures under Title IX. A responsible employee, according to Title IX, includes anyone a student believes could have the authority to take action to redress sexual violence or misconduct.

Supporting the Professional Identities of University Staff in Turbulent Times

T. Renee Ballard and W. Reed Scull

> "There is a Chinese curse which says, 'May [s]he live in interesting times.' Like it or not, we live in interesting times. They are times of danger and uncertainty; but they are also the most creative of any time in the history of mankind."
>
> —Robert F. Kennedy, Day of Affirmation Address, University of Cape Town, June 6, 1966

Like many traditional universities across the United States, the University of Wyoming (UW) is swimming in a sea of change rocked by self- and external criticism. A move for massive budget cuts to cover a $40 million loss of state funding, a rapid succession of university presidents, the arrival of numerous new deans and directors, significant retirements of senior university staff and faculty, and even controversies over institutional marketing campaign slogans have been covered in venues such as *Inside Higher Education* and the *Chronicle of Higher Education*.

It is to our university's credit, we believe, that leaders took the opportunity to solicit the opinions of university faculty and staff about the institutional climate during these "interesting times."

Below we review the university's survey efforts as well as its response to their results. We share our sense of that response's impacts and then offer some practical takeaways for leaders at other institutions. One such takeaway is the development of professional identity. Research on this concept of identity suggests that a more developed sense of that identity affects how a person makes choices and conforms to a work ethic and could directly affect morale.

The survey efforts

Last year UW employees administered two surveys: the Great Colleges to Work for Survey sponsored by the *Chronicle of Higher Education* and ModernThink LLC and the UW Staff Senate's Professional Development Survey. The results of these surveys showcased "certain common areas of concern." Two areas stood out: alarmingly low employee morale and the perception of multiple barriers to professional development at UW. The Staff Senate strongly believed that professional development could help increase employee morale on campus if these barriers were addressed.

The university's response

UW responded to the survey results by arranging several town hall meetings with faculty, staff, and administration. Armed with information from these town hall meetings, the leaders of the two survey groups formed the Strategic Improvement Working Group to address the morale and professional development issues the surveys had raised. This working group quickly began to take the lead on and implement ideas for staff professional development. The Human Resources Department at UW was already working on providing access to LinkedIn Learning for all full-time benefited employees to give them an opportunity for professional development, and managers there redoubled their efforts to make this access happen. The management of the department recognized well the appeal of LinkedIn Learning, as it allowed employees to tie professional development directly to their social media accounts and engage in microlearning.

Impacts of the university response

University HR managers were happy to join forces with the Strategic Improvement Working Group as this was a great way to publicize and increase university buy-in for the LinkedIn Learning product. LinkedIn Learning went live at UW in August 2019, and the HR–Strategic Working Group alliance plans to conduct a survey of the employees who are using the services six months after the program's initial implementation. Per week, the university is currently seeing about 30 courses completed and 1,000 videos watched. HR has also found this tool to be useful in pairing training courses with corrective actions for employees. The next step HR would like to take is to open this product to non-benefitted employees, which comprise a growing proportion of staff and faculty in higher education institutions across the U.S.

Practical takeaways for leaders at other institutions

We are hopeful that the LinkedIn Learning program has helped put UW staff on a more successful path—one on which they see themselves as administrative and educational professionals whose work is essential to university operations, not as mere functionaries. With exposure to supports such as professional development opportunities, one's professional identity forms, whether that formation occurs intentionally or unconsciously.

In a 2009 article published in *Higher Education*, Celia Whitchurch found that in times of austerity and rapid change, universities have called upon staff to engage in work that straddles both academic and administrative support domains. This has created a growing group of what Whitchurch calls "third space" professionals. And expert consensus on the degree to which institutional leaders can support institutional staff consistent with this new "space" is in a developmental stage. Of course, much higher salaries and employee benefits quickly come to mind, but these options are seldom available in times of fiscal turmoil.

We believe that professional development opportunities, thoughtfully developed and deployed, can help move many university staff from an identity as an employee toward seeing the value they bring to the institution as a whole. We suggest that it is this professional identity that will help members of our university staff see their work as contributions to the larger higher education community. It will help the stop focusing on the rapidly passing moment and focus beyond their department, and more consciously and purposefully embrace their likely growing role in the university's educational mission.

Seeing the larger cause in turbulent times challenges all of us, but we know it is a particular task of academic leaders to constantly orient their people and organizations to the educational mission. We suggest to academic leaders that it is exactly times like these that present the greatest opportunities to think expansively—indeed, creatively—about the role of university staff.

Reference

Whitchurch, C. (2009). The rise of the blended professional in higher education: A comparison between the United Kingdom, Australia and the United States. *Higher Education, 58*(3), 407–418. https://doi.org/10.1007/s10734-009-9202-4

Survival: The Impetus for Vigorous Undergraduate Student Recruitment

N. Douglas Lees

Many of our institutions of higher education are presently in a fierce competition to recruit undergraduates. For some of them it is a matter of survival: improve your recruitment outcomes or suffer the fiscal consequences of increasing costs to offer a competitive student experience and incur annual deficits. Institutions that are at particular risk are smaller, stand-alone public colleges and universities and small liberal arts colleges with limited endowments. Large public universities with strong research programs, solid academic reputations, and widespread public support and high-profile private liberal arts colleges have been largely immune from fiscal demise due to enrollment declines, although some will claim they are experiencing some pain. Such institutions are backed by significant public accounts comprised of past excess income, large endowments, and a favorable economy of scale. For example, in 2018 there were 103 US colleges and universities with endowments of over $1 billion. (See this list: https://en.wikipedia.org/wiki/List_of_colleges_and_universities_in_the_United_States_by_endowment.)

Student recruiting at the top colleges and universities

Large state flagship and land grant institutions have not had enrollment challenges thus far, with many of them turning away qualified applicants each year. As major state universities they have an array of professional schools (business, engineering, public health) and other undergraduate programs (music, dance, theater, art), some of which are highly ranked at the national level, that will appeal to students from other states and countries. Because the undergraduate tuition for nonresident students is typically two to three times the resident rate and because many bring diversity to the campus, these students are particularly attractive. Even at nonresident tuition rates, these programs are often less expensive than their similarly ranked, counterpart programs at private institutions.

The upper-level and elite private institutions are also well-positioned to recruit new students in numbers and quality that ensure their goals are met. They are more concerned about the "mix" of students they recruit for each class. They have very healthy (to say the least) endowments that can be tapped to create the right blend of students. The "top" public institutions also recruit as much for the characteristics of the class as they do for the final number of students.

Thus, all these institutions (top public and flagship, elite and upper-level private) are able to maintain enrollments that include many of the very best and most attractive student prospects. These institutions also offer the best of the "extras" (top-ranked athletic programs, great job placement, high percentages of professional and graduate school admissions, etc.) that prospective students and their families seek. Institutions in these categories remain active in student recruiting to stay competitive among their peers and to attract the very best students. In addition, many in this group are growing significantly in enrollment each year and seem limited in their capacity to accommodate more students only by the speed with which they can build new dormitories and other facilities.

Why has student recruiting become so critical?

There are a number of *direct factors* that are responsible for the fiscal squeeze that has resulted in the increased emphasis in student recruitment. Demographics show decreasing numbers of high school graduates in many areas of the US (Bransberger, 2018). This is particularly true in the Midwest and Northeast. In line with the increased diversification in the US, losses are seen very prominently in the white population, with the growth being seen primarily among Hispanic students. Despite recent increases among Hispanic students, the college attendance rate for minority students lags behind that for white students, a reality that translates into fewer applicants in the years to come.

The recently posted 2019 fall-term enrollment estimates from the National Student Clearinghouse Research Center (2019) showed an overall decline of 1.3 percent in the number of students registered in postsecondary institutions. The decline was seen in all institutional types, with four-year public and four-year private institutions decreasing by 1.2 and 0.6 percent, respectively. A deeper dig into the statistics revealed 1.9 and 3.6 percent declines (a total of 36,257 students) in the number of first-year students starting their collegiate life at four-year public and four-year private institutions, respectively. Demographics, coupled with the overall drop in the US higher education attendance rate, means and will continue to result in fewer students from whom to recruit the first-year classes for many of our colleges and universities. Although it is difficult to measure its impact, the current anti-intellectual environment in the US may be a factor in the drop in higher education attendance.

There are also some *indirect factors* that share responsibility for the increased attention being paid to student recruitment. Mounting student debt has received much media attention in the past few years and has resulted in most public institutions "approving" (some voluntary and others imposed by or negotiated with boards or legislatures) low or no tuition increases. Private colleges and universities have moderated tuition increases to address constituent resistance, to demonstrate empathy with students who must borrow to attend, and to avoid the criticism over student debt. Finally, for a number of years state appropriations to higher education have been flat or near flat at best or decreased at worst.

Concurrent with these events, overall campus costs continue to increase at a rate beyond that of inflation. These costs include salary increments for faculty, staff, and other personnel; federal and state-mandated compliance costs; improved security; more pervasive technology; instrumentation (for workplace competitiveness); voluntary efforts to improve diversity and inclusion; new faculty costs (recruiting expenses, salaries and benefits, and start-up costs); and more. The recent emphasis on STEM areas means hiring on the high end salary-wise, and if institutions expect these faculty members to offer cutting-edge education and student training (and to conduct research!), there will be significant start-up costs. Summarizing, we have a decreasing applicant pool; large, powerful universities growing their enrollments; the inability to raise prices to cover full costs; an atmosphere that questions the value of what we offer; no real increase in state support; and increasing internal costs. The only avenue to fiscal survival is to increase student enrollment, including both the number of students recruited and the number retained.

Ways to make your institution more competitive in student recruiting

So how do Local Public University (LPU) and Vanilla Liberal Arts College (VLAC) compete for students with a major public research university and a high-profile liberal arts college? The answer is that *they must promote themselves as (1) distinctive and (2) meeting the needs of targeted subsets of the applicant pool*. The first and obvious thing to do to recruit students is to emphasize what you do best and what makes your institution unique. If you have programs that outperform those of your competitors, don't be shy about touting that in your recruitment efforts. Major Public University may offer two to three hundred degree programs, but there are others not represented in that number. Examples from my school and institution (an LPU) are forensics and neuroscience (both offered collaboratively by Biology and Chemistry and by Biology and Psychology, respectively), philanthropy, medical humanities, race car engineering, and new media. Perhaps you have or could develop a theme-based general education curriculum around an important contemporary topic (e.g., sustainability or world cultures or civility) that would resonate with subsets of students. There would be elements of the topic in all general education courses. Finally, if you have a graduate professional school on your campus, devise a program for undergraduates who are interested in having an experience with the school.

To attract subsets of students to LPU or VLAC, who may otherwise attend the major public university because it is expected of them or all their friends are going there, you may consider taking advantage of your location relative to the competition. If you are in or near an urban environment, you might emphasize the availability of internships or part-time work and the cultural aspects (e.g., diverse population, arts, museums, sports) of city life. If you are in a rural setting, emphasize field studies, outdoor activities, and the beauty of the location. Because your institution is smaller than the competition, you can point to differences in class size; the probably lower cost of attendance; the individual attention that is available; and special programming or support (e.g., undergraduate research, focus on first generation students, peer advising) that may be prominent at your institution.

A future view of US enrollments

The challenge of growing or maintaining enrollments that many of our institutions now face will remain over the next decade, and it will be accompanied by new challenges in retaining the increasing number of less prepared and low-income students who will mark the talent pools of the future. At the end of the decade, a major drop (the "cliff") in the number of high school graduates is projected, which means that the problems facing LPU and VLAC today will grow more dire and move up the hierarchy of our institutions, forcing others to grapple with retention and related issues. In the meantime wealthy institutions will continue to thrive due to their reputations and deep pockets (cash reserves and endowment resources much of which is targeted to student scholarships). LPU and VLAC will be at risk if they can't carve out and recruit distinct student populations within the annual pool of new students. They can achieve this outcome if they effectively market and promote their innovations and distinctiveness. This will be the subject of a future article.

Editor's Note: This article was planned and written before the COVID-19 pandemic. This affliction will result in across-the-board losses in student enrollment in the short term with the possibility of some long-term negative consequences. How long and how deep the losses will be depend on factors (e.g., When will an effective vaccine be available? When will the economy rebound? When will our campuses reopen? Will there be a special government intervention to allow students to continue their educations in the absence of full family employment?) that are largely unknown at this time.

References

Bransberger, P. (2018, July 24). *Demographics, high school graduates & higher education demand* [PowerPoint slides]. https://static1.squarespace.com/static/57f269e19de4bb8a69b470ae/t/5b57353ff950b-7329f3c9856/1532441920461/July+24+2018+PBransberger+Slides+-for+web.pdf

National Student Clearinghouse Research Center. (2019, December 16.) *Fall 2019: Current term enrollment estimates.* http://nscresearchcenter.org/current-term-enrollment-estimates-2019

Effective Strategies for Increasing Undergraduate Student Enrollment

Lauren A. Kay-Beason, Lindsay N. Heinzman, Simon J. Rhodes, and N. Douglas Lees

In a recent *Academic Leader* article, we outlined the need for colleges and universities to increase their efforts in undergraduate student recruiting in order to remain fiscally secure in an environment where the student pool is shrinking. The top public and private universities and colleges will continue to prosper on account of reputation, quality, size, and large cash reserves that include billion-dollar endowments. It is the tiers below these universities that will have to scramble for students. In that article we suggested that these institutions define what distinguishes them (what is particularly excellent and unique about them) and direct their attention, through appropriate marketing strategies, to subsets of the applicant pool that they best serve. Our purpose here is to suggest some strategies for promoting your strengths and uniqueness so that your institution can successfully compete for undergraduate students.

Context

In this article we present approaches, activities, and strategies that the School of Science at Indiana University–Purdue University Indianapolis (IUPUI), our home institution, has successfully employed. We had several goals to fulfill with our marketing initiative, which included reaching out to alumni, enhancing philanthropy, and educating the public at large regarding the academic strength of the institution as well as recruiting undergraduate students. Our active participation in student recruitment started in 2010–11 with the hiring of three individuals for this and related purposes. At the same time, school leadership changed, and within a short period thereafter, the marketing campaign had begun to yield dividends. For the six-year period from 2013–14 through 2018–19, the number of school majors increased by 610 while the campus number, excluding the school results, showed a decrease of 1,700 majors.

The campus environment

The IUPUI campus is located in downtown Indianapolis. A 10-minute walk will get you to the Indiana State House, and a 15-minute walk will get you to the center of the city. Three museums and a zoo border the campus. Indianapolis is home to many sports venues, including those for NFL and NBA franchises, Triple-A baseball, and lower-level professional teams in hockey and soccer. Indianapolis is also home to the NCAA headquarters (located just south of campus) and the world-famous Indianapolis Motor Speedway. In addition, Indianapolis has the other amenities (theaters, symphony, etc.) typical of similar-sized US cities.

We mention the above characteristics because each is a potential lure to an element of each high school graduation class, especially for students not coming from central Indiana. The marketing for the School of Science and the marketing materials coming from the Office of. Admissions both highlight these attractions.

IUPUI has 17 schools, two of which—Engineering & Technology and Science—offer Purdue University degrees. It is also is home to a large array of professional schools, including dentistry, law, and the largest or second-largest (depending on the year that you ask!) medical school in the US. The campus is clearly focused on human health and life sciences. This focus goes beyond IUPUI and includes the central Indiana area.

There are seven departments and two independent degree programs in the School of Science, each of which has a life sciences flavor. Besides Biology, there are Chemistry & Chemical Biology, Computer Science, Earth Sciences, Mathematics, Physics, and Psychology. The two undergraduate programs are Forensic & Investigative Sciences (FIS; fully accredited by the Forensic Science Education Programs Accreditation Commission) and Neuroscience (NS). FIS is the result of a collaborative effort on the parts of Biology and Chemistry & Chemical Biology, and NS is a collaborative program between Biology and Psychology. FIS is unique in the state, and NS programs are uncommon at the undergraduate level.

Beyond distinctive degree programs, Science has additional elements that are used to attract prospective undergraduates. Since IUPUI's formation in 1969, faculty members have mentored undergraduate students in research. At that time they were the only "hands" we had, and our commitment to undergraduate research remains unrelenting today even with the availability of MS and PhD students.

Our environment—health and life sciences—affords our students many opportunities for part-time employment and internships. Internal examples of such opportunities include the Freshman Work Program (FWP) in biology where incoming majors work up to 10 hours per week (for pay) for faculty members or staff. Originally instituted as a retention initiative (Malik & Lees, 2017), it has proven to be very popular with students (some students remain affiliated with their lab for all four years) and their parents thus making it an attractive recruiting tool. Biology has also developed, with the School of Medicine, the Life-Health Sciences Internship (LHSI) program (Malik & Lees, 2017). This program places sophomore or junior students with professional school aspirations in their target school for year-long internships. Undergraduate research, the FWP, and the LHSIs would be things to prominently mention in recruiting materials and during campus visits. Faculty research successes are also highlighted and are routinely accompanied by pictures displaying the entire research group, including identified undergraduates.

The marketing team

The marketing team now consists of four people and works closely with the campus admissions office, the campus communications and marketing office, development, alumni affairs, academic affairs, and the career office. The team consists of the marketing director, a communications staff member, a web developer, and a recruiter. *We recommend that the director of the recruiting effort be trained or highly experienced in both marketing and student recruiting.* The team also uses current undergraduate students in recruiting. These students, called ambassadors, are a mix of volunteers completing institutional service obligations and student hourly workers. The ambassadors serve several roles that we will discuss later, but for now suffice to say that they are close enough in age to be peers to prospective students and thus can influence their decisions to attend the institution. *We recommend that current undergraduate students be a part of the recruitment effort.*

The substance of our message

Our unofficial school slogan is "We graduate success stories," so we use individual examples of student successes in our printed and electronic materials. Because success comes in many forms, these materials can feature stories of (among other things) outstanding academic performance, research findings, significant engagement activities, scholarship recipients, and post-graduation admissions. Likewise, faculty successes—whether high-profile research (e.g., on addictions or obesity) or large grant awards—are featured with pictures of the research group, which, again, has undergraduate members.

Converting these successes into stories suitable for a website is the responsibility of the marketing team's communications member. On occasions when a story is deemed of broad general interest, we call upon the expertise of this individual again to develop a plan for reaching the external media. Versions of the stories are also prepared for emails to alumni and for hard-copy materials, such as brochures.

The sources of materials for these stories are many. They include the academic affairs (student achievements and awards); development (large gifts, especially student scholarships); and alumni (their career successes) offices as well as academic departments including faculty (new grants, research breakthroughs, teaching innovations, contributions of undergraduate students). Academic departments are eager to share this information.

Technology

The marketing team uses technology extensively to deliver its message efficiently and effectively and communicate with prospective students in ways they expect. The team uses a customer relationship management tool to send out timed messages to all or to subsets of prospective students. Marketing uses is the same tool used by the Office of Admissions, thus allowing our team to see all communications with prospective students. Because a growing number of students use social media to help make their college choices, the school also has Facebook, Twitter, Instagram, and email accounts that it uses to correspond with prospective students.

The campus visit

This is a key step to successful recruiting. The campus visit represents the first face-to-face meeting between school representatives and the student prospects. These days' events, which can vary depending on a number of factors, are carefully coordinated with the Office of Admissions. This office focuses on campus-level topics—such as housing, parking, and financial aid—for part of the day. The science recruiter then takes students to the school, where they tour research labs and meet with faculty, advisors, and current students. Here they learn about the curricula, degree options, undergraduate research, clubs, and the like and are taken on tours through research labs where they are greeted by faculty and their current research students. A popular highlight of some student visits is a panel, comprised of our student ambassadors, that presents and takes questions on "what it is like to be a student in the School of Science." For recruiting the class beginning in fall 2020, the marketing team will be converting the campus visit to a virtual visit in order to accommodate the restrictions resulting from the COVID-19 pandemic.

Before departing each prospective student receives a memento of the institution and the school. It may be a backpack, a water bottle, or a pen (all with the appropriate branding) that serves as reminder of our continued interest in them as they prepare to make that final decision. Shortly thereafter each prospect receives a handwritten note or an email from a student ambassador that thanks them for attending and invites any questions that may arise.

Close collaboration between admissions and the school team is critical in assuring that accurate, complete, non-duplicative information is provided to students. We further recommend that the team make certain that the research labs are selected on the basis of dependability and enthusiasm for student recruiting.

Reference

Malik, D. J., & Lees, N. D. (2017). Department and school programs that increase student retention, success and engagement. *Academic Leader, 33*(8), 4–5. https://www.academic-leader.com/topics/students/programs-that-increase-student-retention-success-and-engagement

A Challenge to Higher Education Leaders in the Wake of a Social Injustice Crisis

Tanjula Petty

Often I find myself writing and providing leadership strategies to assist academic leaders on their respective journeys in higher education. Thus, now I find myself distraught as we operate in the face of an increasingly unbearable reality of social injustice. As higher education administrators we have a role and responsibility to model principles of civility, respect, and understanding for our faculty, staff, and students. Importantly, we must demonstrate these same tenets in our wider community. Countless college and university mission statements include the terms *community, collaboration*, and *diversity*. We must do more than use the terms; we must demonstrate these ideas through our actions as these terms alone do not allow institutions to stand boldly and support social justice for all marginalized groups.

Social justice is relevant to many facets of higher education institutions: academics, athletics, finances, facilities, career services, disability services—the list goes on. As academic leaders we must recognize that every aspect of our leadership principles affects social justice on our campuses. Moreover, it is our obligation to embody inclusivity, embrace diversity, and educate others about their power and their voices. As academic administrators we must do our due diligence to instill in our students an understanding about the basic rights to life and liberty that all people possess, regardless of race, religion, gender identity, sexual orientation, or ethnicity. We must position ourselves to fight for systemic change in our institutions to ensure a sustainable future for our diverse student populations and their successors. Our black students are due the opportunity to live in freedom and security, not in fear.

In the aftermath of the murder of George Floyd, many of our students are confronting a variety of emotions, including confusion, fury, outrage, pain, and sadness, as they seek clarity, sympathy, and understanding. They have watched as insular hate has driven the deepest wedge in this country that many of us have witnessed in our lifetimes.

At this point in my career, I am fortunate enough to have gained experience at historically black colleges, predominantly white institutions, four-year and two-year institutions. While all intuitions are committed to educating students, my experiences lead me to say that HBCUs must "move differently" to serve and support their students. HBCUs have a significant role as they were the first institutions to provide African American students with the opportunity to obtain full access to a college education, without barriers to entry. Today, HBCUs are still an integral part of the higher education experience for African American students. They provide opportunities of access to first-generation and disadvantaged students. They have been the lifeline for many students who would otherwise not have a chance to receive a postsecondary education.

Notably, HBCUs have been able to give a breath of life to many disadvantaged, first-generation, and underserved African American students. This breath of life consists of more than just educational opportunities and academic support; it also includes career pathways, national and international internship opportunities, and exposure to a culturally diverse group of faculty and students, which allows a person to flourish creatively, intellectually, and socially as part of a larger African American community. Unfortunately, this breath of life is also given in the country of "I can't breathe"—the fateful and final words of both Eric Gardner and George Floyd, words many African Americans chant to bring attention to their social asphyxiation in the face of systemic racial injustice.

Although I and many others have immense pride in HBCUs—after all, we are products of them—it is immensely difficult to watch where we are as a country. For we work tirelessly to provide the breath of life for our students through testaments of encouragement and hope. Consequently, it is unfortunate they have to continue to witness the ugly face of racism rear its head over and over again, with no justice being served. Black people endure racism and discrimination that leads to their deaths year after year at the hands of white police officers, who take an oath to protect and serve. We can be murdered and justice not be served. Think of the names: Trayvon Martin, Michael Brown, Laquan McDonald, Tamir Rice, Walter Scott,

Freddie Gray, Sandra Bland, Philandro Castile, Botham Jean, Ahmaud Arbery, and Breonna Taylor—to say nothing of the many others whose deaths have not attracted media attention. These deaths are constant reminders of the discrimination, intolerance, and other barriers to social justice that have burdened African Americans for far too long. Incident after incident, year after year, "liberty and justice for all" escape us while we choke to death because we cannot breathe. There is much work to be done to address the racial injustices and inequities that African Americans face.

As the mother of a black man, I stop breathing every time my son leaves my presence. I choke and almost suffocate because I do not know what is on the other side of the door. As an academic administrator, each time we confer degrees and release highly educated black males who are ready to change the world, it should be a joy, yet I stop breathing. My heart stops each time I hear of another killing. Similarly, many of us in higher education, regardless of race, take quickly to our students. We grow to love and adore them. Indeed, they become a part of our extended families. They become our sons and daughters.

So I ask my colleagues in higher education: How are you using your voice to stand against the injustices that are happening across the country, in your states, in your cities, or on your campuses? As you are aware, our students are watching how we use our resources and voices to stand up for them against the injustices that are occurring. As leaders in higher education, we have more to think about than moving the needle on enrollment, retention, graduation, or growing our endowment dollars. We are being called on to place our integrity and values above all else. It is time to demonstrate that we care about our students and will stand up and defend their civil rights and their basic human dignity by any means necessary. If we are going to lead our universities and colleges through these atrocious times, we must stand together to support our students, so that they all can begin to breathe and live in a society that is not suffocating and killing them. I will leave you with this action item: How will you give your students breath? Isn't that what higher education is about?

PART II
Leading Through Conflict

Creating Dialogue in the Interest of Social Justice on Campus

Edna B. Chun and Alvin Evans

In a polarized national climate, free speech and First Amendment protections have drawn increasing attention on college campuses. With the advent of open white nationalism, expressions of white supremacy, and the potential for hate speech, campuses have sought to protect student safety and guard against the harassment of minoritized students. As the American Civil Liberties Union (ACLU) indicates, "An open society depends on liberal education, and the whole enterprise of liberal education is founded on the principle of free speech." At the same time, however, the ACLU warns that the First Amendment does not protect behavior that involves "targeted harassment or threats, or that creates a pervasively hostile environment for vulnerable students." Similarly, in its 1992 statement on "Freedom of Expression and Campus Speech Codes," the American Association of University Professors (AAUP) indicates that freedom of thought and expression are essential to institutions of higher learning but warns that civility is fragile and can easily be destroyed.

Balancing the interests of free speech with these concerns has become increasingly difficult. According to a recent 100-page report issued by PEN America (2019), a national political debate has erupted over free speech, hate speech, and the attainment of diversity and inclusion. The report asks how institutions of higher education can uphold democratic values in a demographically diverse country while attempting to address legacies of racial exclusion and bigotry.

Weighing in on issues of free speech, President Trump's recent executive order requires federal grant-making agencies ensure that institutions receiving federal research funds comply with laws and regulations that involve free academic inquiry. The Trump administration has filed statements of interest in five free-speech lawsuits against the University of Iowa, the University of Michigan, Los Angeles Pierce College, Georgia Gwinnett College, and the University of California, Berkeley (Mangan 2019b).

At times, the potential for volatile demonstrations has led colleges and universities to cancel speaker appearances at the last minute. Part of the ongoing dilemma campus leaders face lies in the need to balance engagement of different parties in constructive debate with the safety and protection of all concerned. How, then, can academic leaders create engagement in civil discourse on contested issues and promote dialogue without creating hostile environments? And how does free speech conducted in a civil and nonthreatening manner promote the interests of a democratic society and student learning regarding social justice?

To address these perplexing questions, take, for example, Middlebury College's last-minute cancellation of a planned public event featuring Ryszard Legutko, a right-wing Polish politician who had expressed antigay views. Middlebury indicates that its concerns escalated as estimates of attendance increased to more than 500 and the potential for demonstrations increased. Legutko, a professor of philosophy at the Jagiellonian University in Kraków, had been invited by the Alexander Hamilton Forum and was apparently still in his hotel room when the cancellation occurred. Matthew Dickinson, a tenured political science professor at Middlebury, learned of the cancellation from his students at 1:30 p.m. Not wanting to make any students uncomfortable, he took a secret poll to see whether his students wanted to invite Legutko to their class, and they voted in favor of it. While waiting for Legutko to arrive, students formulated questions and researched issues. Dozens of other students soon entered the classroom to join the discussion, and their interactions with Legutko were livestreamed on Facebook. Dickinson viewed the dialogue as "a teaching moment," describing the encounter as "one of the best teaching experiences I've had" (Mangan 2019a).

Recall how Middlebury had previously experienced the painful racial divide that is currently bifurcating American society. In 2017, a student group called the American Enterprise Institute Club sponsored a lecture by Charles Murray. Murray is coauthor of the controversial *The Bell Curve*, which attempts to link social and economic inequality and IQ test scores to genetic differences. The lecture was shut down amid disruption by student activists. Protesters climbed on and rocked the car in which Murray and Professor Allison Stanger, the faculty facilitator and a liberal professor, were seated. After recovering from whiplash and a concussion she experienced when shoved by protesters in the incident, Stanger (2017) reflected: "I hear and understand the righteous anger of many of those who shouted us down. I know that many students felt they were standing up to protect marginalized people who have been demeaned or even threatened under the guise of free speech."

Given this controversial incident and the challenges it presented, the interactions with Ryszard Legutko at Middlebury illustrate the fragility of maintaining civil discourse on controversial issues. The discussion facilitated by Professor Dickinson underscores the delicate nature of interactions on contentious issues. Yet it also highlights the potential for students to experience cognitive dissonance when they encounter different and antithetical perspectives. As we point out in *Rethinking Cultural Competence in Higher Education: An Ecological Framework for Student Development* (Jossey-Bass, 2016), cognitive dissonance that results from encountering different views and perspectives can stimulate cognitive growth, especially during one's undergraduate years. Individuals must attempt to reconcile new and often conflicting information with their existing views. The progressive process of addressing conflicting perspectives can lead to greater cognitive understanding and perceived opportunity as individuals themselves become change agents and innovators on the front lines of diversity and inclusion.

In walking the fine line between freedom of expression and protecting the interests of vulnerable students, when opportunities for engagement with diverse and even conflicting perspectives promote civil discourse, such discussions may enhance the process of student learning and civic participation. Although discomfort may result, as long as speakers do not engage in hateful or violent speech or harass or silence individuals or groups, the cognitive dissonance arising from sharply different perspectives can generate deep reflection that ultimately enriches the educational experience. While seemingly counterintuitive, the iterative process of engagement and civil dialogue may actually increase the potential for realizing an inclusive educational environment in support of social justice.

References

American Civil Liberties Union. n.d. "Speech on Campus." Accessed April 24, 2019. https://www.aclu.org/other/speech-campus.

American Association of University Professors. 1992. "On Freedom of Expression and Campus Speech Codes." https://www.aaup.org/report/freedom-expression-and-campus-speech-codes.

Mangan, Katherine. 2019a. "Controversial Speaker, His Event Canceled by Middlebury College, Finds an Audience in a Campus Seminar." *Chron-*

icle of Higher Education, April 15, 2019. https://www.chronicle.com/article/Controversial-Speaker-His/246152.

Mangan, Katherine. 2019b. "If There Is a Free-Speech 'Crisis' on Campus, PEN American Says, Lawmakers Are Making It Worse." *Chronicle of Higher Education*, April 24, 2019. https://www.chronicle.com/article/If-There-Is-a-Free-Speech/246031.

PEN America. 2019. *Chasm in the Classroom: Campus Free Speech in a Divided America*. https://pen.org/wp-content/uploads/2019/04/2019-PEN-Chasm-in-the-Classroom-04.25.pdf.

Stanger, Allison. 2017. "Understanding the Angry Mob at Middlebury That Gave Me a Concussion." *New York Times*, March 13, 2017. https://www.nytimes.com/2017/03/13/opinion/understanding-the-angry-mob-that-gave-me-a-concussion.html.

Campus Civility Project: Emotionally Intelligent Conversations

Elizabeth Lewis and Emily Moore

Because divisive national political rhetoric has spilled over into higher education, Wake Technical Community College launched the Campus Civility Project: Emotionally Intelligent Conversations in 2017. This project was part of a Campus Compact Fund for Positive Engagement mini-grant, focusing on improving civil discourse among Wake Tech students, faculty, and staff. Creating an environment of civility and respect "is a college-wide responsibility including the words and actions of administrators, faculty, staff, and students. It must be ongoing and interactive" (Popovics, 2014). To reach all areas, levels, and members of the college, the Campus Civility Project was a collaborative effort led by a provost, dean, department head, and faculty member. Through emotional intelligence training, online professional development, assimilation in course curriculum, student promotional video creation, and tailoring training to specialized groups, the Campus Civility Project has successfully reached hundreds of administrators, faculty, staff, and students in less than two years.

Emotional intelligence training

To first establish a strong foundation of knowledge as project leads, we developed our awareness and comprehension of elements of civil discourse by each completing and ultimately becoming certified in administering the Emotional Quotient Inventory (EQ-i 2.0). The EQ-i 2.0 "is the world's leading assessment tool used for assessing emotional and social intelligence"; upon completion, users receive a report outlining their scores in "15 competencies, grouped into five composite areas: Self-Perception, Self-Expression, Interpersonal, Decision Making and Stress Management" (EITC, 2019).

Through the guidance of a coach and a two-day comprehensive workshop, we used the data and feedback from our individual reports to identify, understand, develop, and refine our distinctive strengths and weaknesses in emotional and social intelligence. By the end of our training, we acquired a thorough understanding of the strengths each team lead could bring to the various components of our project, allowing for thoughtful, productive collaboration.

Online training

The second phase of the Campus Civility Project was the creation of a training course designed to increase a core group of Wake Tech stakeholders' ability to demonstrate and facilitate emotionally intelligent conversations. This goal was based on research providing evidence of the positive correlation between increased emotional intelligence and better social relationships (Schutte, Malouff, & Thorsteinsson, 2013). Initially, we conceived of this training as several in-person training sessions for administrators, faculty, staff, and students. As the team began to build the training course, however, we realized that an online format would allow us to reach a greater number of stakeholders. As a result, we decided to create an online course in our learning management system (LMS) with modules for faculty and staff. These modules can also be copied directly into instructors' course shells through our LMS and thus delivered virtually to students. Considering the core elements of emotional intelligence that we learned during the EQ-i 2.0 certification program, the team decided to focus on two main areas of emotional intelligence—assertiveness and empathy—as the foundation of the lessons created for the online course. We chose these two skills because they are necessary for individuals in civil conversations to understand others (empathy) and make themselves understood (assertiveness). The online course consisted of two lessons, one on each skill, with instructional slides, videos, quizzes, and discussion boards in each lesson. We designed course materials to appeal to a wide audience. Examples include a Brené Brown video on empathy (The RSA, 2013) and a Mayo Clinic article on assertiveness (Mayo Clinic Staff, 2017). We initially shared the online course with instructors in the Arts, Humanities, and Social Sciences Division at Wake Tech and eventually with faculty, staff, and students throughout the college. More than 90 faculty and staff members have enrolled in the online course, and the online modules have reached over 500 students.

Course integration

In addition to the online course, the team integrated the training modules into seated courses. During this training, students completed the coursework and then engaged in an application activity. Instructors paired students with opposing views on a topic and directed them to discuss the topic using civil conversation techniques. The students were given a list of sentence starters to help them demonstrate empathy and assertiveness during these conversations across difference. Students who participated in this activity were asked to reflect on their experiences. Representative student comments included the following: "Society should focus less on who is wrong versus who is right. We should be more focused on listening where the other person is coming from and trying to find the best solution for everyone" and "Being able to experience and listen to someone else's viewpoints made me feel and be more accepting."

Student video integration

From the initial group of student participants, we recruited volunteers with divergent beliefs about current political and social issues to participate in videotaped dialogues during February of 2018. Using skills developed during the emotional intelligence training, they discussed their perspectives on controversial issues with each other and demonstrated how to respond to differences in a civil and productive manner. We combined excerpts from these sessions into a short video during April 2018 (Wake Tech Instructional, 2018). We shared this video in classrooms across our campuses, in online classes including the Campus Civility Project course, and on our college website. In addition, we shared the video with the national Campus Compact organization as part of the final Fund for Positive Engagement report.

Customized training

After one year of implementation, popularity surrounding the Campus Civility Project increased, resulting in faculty and staff across the college reaching out for more information about and inclusion in the online training. Also, Wake Tech's Office of the Registrar specifically requested in-person, specialized civility training in handling student and parent complaints and invited us to lead a customized, two-hour session at their office's spring professional development retreat. In preparation for the seated session, we asked that the attendees complete the two-hour online training course. Using their responses to the reflection questions on the course shell, we then designed the seated session as a customized extension of the material in the online course, complete with relevant student and parent scenarios for contemplation and group discussion. We gave participants the opportunity to openly share their concerns, frustrations, and potential techniques in handling these matters. Participants left with tools and strategies to promote civil discourse for emotionally intelligent communication with parents, students, and one another.

Conclusion

The Campus Civility Project has successfully helped numerous administrators, faculty, staff, and students both in and outside of Wake Tech. In fact, as a result of the Campus Civility Project, almost 90 percent of Wake Tech participants report feeling more confident about engaging in civil conversation with people who hold opposing views. Eager to spread this confidence and increase awareness regarding the importance of campus civility, we have shared our project with other community colleges and four-year colleges and universities at local and national conferences. During these presentations, we provide participants with strategies, resources, and tools, as well as our contact information for informal consulting and help with troubleshooting, so that they may successfully tailor and implement this initiative at their respective institutions. We firmly agree that "colleges cannot exist, untainted, in a context of incivility, violence, and bigotry" (Morris, 2016) and hope other institutions of higher education will adopt their own campus civility projects to promote thoughtful, productive, and emotionally intelligent discourse.

References

EITC. (2019). What is the EQ-i 2.0? Retrieved from https://www.eitrainingcompany.com/eq-i

Mayo Clinic Staff. (2017, May 9). Being assertive: Reduce stress, communicate better. Retrieved from https://www.mayoclinic.org/healthy-lifestyle/stress-management/in-depth/assertive/art-20044644

Morris, L. V. (2016). Collective action for civil discourse. *Innovative Higher Education, 41*(5), 361–363. https://doi.org/10.1007/s10755-016-9376-5

Popovics, J. A. (2014). Civility on community college campuses: A shared responsibility. *College Student Journal, 48*(1), 130–132.

The RSA. (2013, December 10). *Brené Brown on empathy* [Video file]. Retrieved from https://www.youtube.com/watch?v=1Evwgu369Jw

Schutte, N. S., Malouff, J. M., & Thorsteinsson, E. B. (2013). Increasing emotional intelligence through training: Current status and future directions. *International Journal of Emotional Education, 5*(1), 56–72. Retrieved from https://core.ac.uk/download/pdf/26812358.pdf

Wake Tech Instructional. (2018, April 28). *Wake Tech campus -civility video* [Video file]. Retrieved from https://www.youtube.com/watch?time_continue=1&v=cbGZA_CKrr8

President-Faculty Relations: A Dean's Dilemma?

Thomas R. McDaniel

The situation: You are an academic dean. Your president is one of the new-breed leaders, a nonacademic administrator whose expertise is in business management, alumni affairs, social life, or development. Further, your faculty is a highly organized cohort of professionals who have the security of a tenure system and the strong leadership of a faculty senate. Now your president, in an effort to establish better communication and rapport with faculty, is meeting with individual faculty members, academic departments, and the faculty senate. Do you see a dilemma in your future?

The scenario above is hardly hypothetical. Increasingly, college presidents come from outside the academy, faculties are highly organized and political, and academic leaders advocate communication and "flat" or horizontal decision-making mechanisms. These evolutions in management theory and practice put the administrative role of the dean, the quintessential middle manager, at peril. At the least, deans need to think about how best to accommodate the increased interaction between faculty and president and to make communication a positive experience for everyone.

The concept of "crisis"

We who spend much of our time in the middle know well the challenge of resolving conflicts. We also recall that the Chinese symbol for *crisis* is a combination of the characters for *danger* and *opportunity*. The desire of both presidents and professors to strengthen relations can constitute dangers and opportunities aplenty. Long gone are the days when a dean might recite the dean's dictum: "My job is to keep the president from *thinking* and the faculty from *talking*." (Or is it the other way around?) To succeed in an era when presidents and professors seek common ground, with or without the involvement of the dean, deans must find ways to minimize dangers and maximize opportunities. Otherwise, they will find life in the middle to be one crisis after another.

In my years as a professor and an administrator, I've had opportunities to assess president-faculty relations and to reflect on the dynamics of such relationships. I have been a professor, an academic dean, and an interim president. I seem to be blessed (cursed?) with an ability to sympathize with conflicting points of view, partly because I understand that where you stand depends on where you sit. Because I have sat in many different seats, I can appreciate almost every point of view. That doesn't make solving crises any easier.

The dean's dilemma

As middle manager, deans have the difficult task of communicating faculty needs to presidents and boards while communicating institutional policies and priorities from the top administrative positions to faculty and staff. Unlike some classic business or military chains of command, colleges have shared decision-making processes, which assign distinct spheres of authority to the board, administration, and faculty. The dean's authority is rarely absolute and is often vaguely defined in college management models and faculty handbooks. In fact, a dean "rules" the faculty only by the consent of the governed and with respect and goodwill earned by fair and faithful leadership. One leads the faculty by helping them achieve their best goals, by bringing them together to solve problems and chart new directions, and by skillful consensus building. Part pastor and part policeman, the dean is lost without human relation skills.

Dilemmas, then, assail deans who fail to listen well, refuse to compromise when good sense and good policy require it, or run roughshod over the sensibilities of individual faculty members. But deans also need to take stands, make decisions, and enforce institutional policies. Presidents can complicate the delicate balances and processes that deans and faculties have worked out over the years to promote a relatively amicable and collegial relationship unique to the academic workplace.

The president's laudable intentions can result in an intensified triangulation that creates conflict and confusion. If, say, the president has "heard" a faculty complaint about another faculty member, does that imply "support" for the complainant? If the president asks the dean to "address" the concern, does that require the dean to support the complainant? Are presidents more likely to micromanage the faculty and faculty to lobby the president for pet projects?

Solutions

So, what's a dean to do? While I have no simple solutions to offer, I do think deans can mitigate middle management crises emanating from this triangulation of president, faculty, and dean. Indeed, with some thought, imagination, and planning, a skillful dean can harness the synergy of triangulation and turn what looks like a crisis into an opportunity. When a president wants to establish communication or collaboration or connection with the faculty, a dean might follow with one or more of these approaches:

- **Reevaluate your relationship with the president.** First, be sure that you enjoy the confidence of the president and that your effectiveness with the faculty is not at issue. Next, make sure you and the president have discussed all the dynamics of triangulation and the ground rules you will follow to avoid end runs, divide-and-conquer strategies or other unintended consequences of president-faculty relations. Finally, be sure that you and the president have a common understanding of the goals of such communications and the methods of follow-up.
- **Reinvent your role as dean.** A dean's authority often is more personal than positional (and vaguely defined). Perhaps you need to work more closely with faculty senate leaders—or more effectively with your president to identify academic needs, issues, and priorities. Perhaps you should arrange more conferences for the president and you with key faculty in each academic department. A dean's authority is limited, but their autonomy is immense.
- **Reestablish your reputation for open communications.** Communication is not a zero-sum process. If the president wants more communication with the faculty, that does not mean you should have less. Do you invite open communication by word and deed? Do you get out on campus and into faculty workspaces (including classrooms) with regularity? Do you need to remind yourself that your leadership depends on your availability, your ability to hear and appreciate individual concerns, and your responsiveness? The battle scars of deaning can dull our sensitivities and undermine our communication skills.

Deans and other middle managers can fall victim to the dangers of president-faculty relations or find the opportunities every crisis or dilemma creates to become more versatile, more creative academic leaders. The choice is ours.

Managing Conflict: Please Don't Leave

Robert E. Cipriano

Spoiler alert: there will be no strategy on how to solve this dilemma . . . yet.

Research suggests that 80 percent of decisions made in institutions of higher education in the United States are made at the department level. Of the approximately 80,000 department chairs, a full 20 percent leave their positions each year. The number one reason chairs list for leaving their chairpersonship is because of noncollegial, uncivil faculty members. In an ongoing 11-year study of more than 2,100 chairs that I and my colleague Richard Riccardi have conducted, managing conflict has consistently been the second or third most important skill/competency that chairs have said they needed to be an effective chair. This is interesting in view of the fact that more than 96 percent of chairs have never been trained or educated in serving as a chair. In fact, in 2017 not one chair in 153 indicated that he or she had education and/or training in serving as chair.

Most people reading this article have probably experienced the toxicity and poisonousness behavior of a person in their department. Incivility in the workplace may be subtle, but its effects are not. The following are signs of incivility, and this is not an exhaustive list:
- Use of condescending tone
- Interruptions
- Treating people as invisible
- Unprofessional terms of address
- Increased levels of stress
- Turnover intentions
- Counterproductive work behavior
- Decreased levels of job satisfaction, actual performance, and

organizational commitment
- Refusal to collaborate with faculty and students

People who are treated poorly often disengage from any and all participation in department functions (e.g., refusing to serve on committees, not advising students, not caring about the department, speaking critically to professionals and students about the department, etc.). Note that people tend to overperform when they are happy and look forward to coming to work and underperform when they are not happy.

What would you do?

You are the chair of a department of 11 faculty members. Dr. Julia Appleby is your most outstanding professor. She is a tenured associate professor who has been in the department for seven years. She regularly publishes in the most prestigious journals in the field, is an outstanding teacher, and serves on five university-wide committees and four department committees. She is also the project director of a large five-year US Department of Education federal grant of $500,000, which is in the second year of the grant. This grant supports your department's graduate program through scholarships for students. Julia e-mails you and says she must speak with you the next morning. The two of you meet in your office, and after the usual pleasantries, she indicates that she will be leaving the university the first chance she gets. She is a finalist at two universities that are your major competitors. Further, she has spoken with the project officer for the grant and she will be able to "take the grant" with her when she leaves. You are dumbstruck and bewildered. You desperately do not want to lose this valuable colleague. Julia states that she cannot take the abuse and noncollegial/uncivil behavior that Dr. Williams shows toward her. He refuses to collaborate, tells students she is incompetent, is downright nasty to her, and belittles her every chance he gets. You are grasping for a solution.

So, what do you do?

"It is that civil conversation—tough, open, principled—between and among all members and parts of the institution that must be preserved. If it is, a community is patiently built. If it is not, the place degenerates into a center of crisis management and competing special interests. What must be open and free is the conversation between young and young, young and old, scholar and scholar, present and past—the sound of voices straining out the truth."

—A. Bartlett Giamatti, *A Free and Ordered Space* (1989), p. 45

Positive Effects of Conflict

Robert E. Cipriano

> *If we could read the secret history of our enemies,*
> *we should find in each man's life sorrow and*
> *suffering enough to disarm all hostility.*
>
> —Henry Wadsworth Longfellow

Conflict is inevitable—it is the natural outcome of human interaction. Anger, grudges, hurt, and blame are not inevitable. Being disrespectful and uncivil is a conscience choice. Conflict is the result of competing ideas or options; conflict occurs because of individual differences. Destructive conflict causes inefficiency. There are many reasons for departmental conflict to occur within institutions of higher education: jealousy, power. Status, money, perceived hurts or slights, convenience, easy scapegoat, personality disorders, ghosts of the past, get-even time, put the heat on him takes the heat off me, and equity issues.

Conflict can be positive. It can improve problem solving, clarify issues, increase participant involvement and commitment, and result in a better decision or outcome. Conflict can be managed. There are conflict-management skills and techniques that exist. Conflict resolution is not the same as conflict management. Chairs should not strive to resolve conflicts (even if we could) because a conflict-free environment would be one so homogeneous it could become not optimally innovative or productive. Members of the academy are well versed in analytical thinking and are passionate in verbalizing their thoughts. Divergent thinking enhances the ability to find solutions to a problem. All people in the department—from graduate assistants up to and including full professors—should have opportunities to express their thoughts *respectfully* without fear of retaliation. A healthy, trustful climate in the department sets the tone for conducting department business in a constructive manner. Recognize, however, that problems will not go away by themselves.

The department chair plays a major and important role in managing conflict within the department. A chair's positive day-to-day interaction with faculty members, staff, and students can minimize destructive conflict. This daily interface can alert the chair to any cues that may signal a brewing conflict. Although chairs are not skilled in crystal-ball reading, they should be able to accurately predict potential conflicts and be ready to intervene when needed. This will be greatly facilitated if the chair walks the halls and interacts with faculty members, staff, and students on a daily basis. Department chairs, like the majority of people, do not like to manage conflict. However, it is an essential part of the role and responsibility of chairs. Apparently, managing conflict is becoming more of a need in higher education. It is very important that chairs develop a good support system. Chairs should seek out colleagues in the university to talk to and get good advice (Cipriano, 2011).

Higgerson (1996) wrote that "if mutual trust exists among colleagues, and faculty air differences openly and constructively, there is less opportunity for destructive conflicts to escalate because individuals are less prone to perceive differences of opinion as personal attacks or components of some hidden agenda." Mutual respect and trust are significant cornerstones in facilitating an approach to managing conflict.

Managing a conflict is based on a clear understanding of what the dispute is really about. Good communication and engagement are keys to successfully managing conflict. When issues are not addressed quickly tension is heightened, resolution is delayed, and collateral damage is increased. The best approach to managing conflict is when the issues are handled in an informal way. Many more problems ensue when letters are written and copies are distributed to others. People than are "professionally obligated" to respond in writing to the allegations put forth in the initial letter. When people are criticized, fairly or unfairly, and the criticism is in the form of an "official" letter, they have elephantine memories. In the final analysis, conflict management is directed toward reducing destructive conflict while allowing for the existence of constructive conflict. Communication, verbal and nonverbal, is the single most important ingredient to managing conflict.

References

Cipriano, R. E. (2011). *Facilitating a collegial department in higher education: Strategies for success.* San Francisco, CA: Jossey-Bass.

Higgerson, M. L. (1996). *Communication skills for department chairs.* Bolton, MA: Anker Publishing.

Managing, Not Eliminating, Intradepartmental Conflict

Academic leaders cannot resolve all intradepartmental disputes, but they can become better at analyzing and managing the sources of conflict to reduce the possibility of long-term negative consequences from conflict.

Conflict is inevitable and is not necessarily negative, says Peter Shedd, professor of legal studies in the Terry College of Business at the University of Georgia. "I make the comparison to children. Brothers and sisters can fight like cats and dogs, and I've often wondered and asked colleagues, 'Why is it that siblings feel comfortable fighting in the family setting?' I think the fundamental reason is that they are secure in that relationship. They know that nothing they say to one another is going to rupture the sibling relationship. Tenured faculty are also secure in their relationship. It gives them a degree of freedom to feel comfortable creating conflict," Shedd says.

Shedd also points out that conflict is an important part of the academic culture. "We cannot expect in any environment, particularly in the academic environment where ideas are at the core of what we are about, to say we want an environment with no conflict. If that's our goal we're going to take all the richness out of the environment. Instead, we should be looking at how to manage conflict, not how to do away with it."

Conflict can come from everyday things like class schedules and office assignments and more serious matters like salary increases and tenure denials, and the process for managing disputes runs the gamut from informal conversation and negotiation to formal adversarial resolution processes like mediation and court proceedings. Academic leaders should try to manage conflict with informal processes when possible, Shedd says.

Communication is the key to keeping conflicts manageable in informal ways, and certainly there are communication and management styles that should be avoided. For example, when a faculty member questions his class schedule, a response such as, "I'm in charge. Don't buck me," from an authoritarian leader might color all future interactions between the leader and the faculty member. If the faculty member doesn't get the resources he asks for or doesn't hear an adequate explanation as to why he isn't getting them, he will be more likely to file a formal grievance than if the leader took the time to explain the situation, Shedd says.

It's also important to be accessible to faculty who want to discuss an issue. "When the faculty want to be heard, it's wonderful for the department chair to take the phone off the hook and say, 'OK, let's visit,' as opposed to saying, 'You don't have an appointment,'" Shedd says.

Because of the potential for formal grievance processes, including lawsuits, academic leaders often feel the need to document each conversation related to conflict, but Shedd warns about taking this too far. "If as a faculty member I felt that everything I was saying was going into a notebook, I'm going begin to shut down and be less willing to resolve things in an amicable way," Shedd says.

In some instances, the faculty member may ask to record conversations with his or her chair. How a chair handles this request will depend on the situation and the parties involved. "The response is either, 'That's OK' because you're willing to stand by anything you say or you say, 'No. That's contrary to the kind of conversation I want to have,'" Shedd says.

Regardless of how the conversation takes place, the parties should talk about the situation so they can try to understand each other's perspective. Although academic leaders are asked to manage conflict, Shedd believes that faculty also need to be prepared to do their part in managing conflict. "In many ways we're asking administrators to be thoughtful enough to not only have thought the conflict through from their perspective but to then become educators about helping the opposing party to approach this conflict in a way that makes sense," Shedd says.

In some instances, it helps to make the conflict public but without pointing the finger at a particular person. If the conflict is universal, such as misgivings about resource allocation, it helps if the department chair explains how the resources will be allocated and why. This information can help reduce conflict or give the department chair principles to come back to if conflict continues. "I think it's a horrible mistake to say, 'I want to talk about allocation of resources because Rob over here has been complaining about not getting his fair share,'" Shedd says.

However, the department chair might wish to alert the individual faculty member who brought up the issue and give him or her the opportunity to speak about it, Shedd says.

Bringing up a conflict in a faculty meeting can help faculty understand why certain decisions had to be made, but it also can cause the department chair to reexamine his or her views. The chair has to be self-confident enough to be willing to listen and even change his or her views as long as it doesn't go against something that is fundamentally critical to his or her position, Shedd says.

There are also times to stand firm. Chairs are understandably leery of escalation of conflict but they have to consider what is critically important to the department. "If the conflict is ripping or trying to tear away those fundamental principles, it's really the chair's responsibility to stand firm. You don't want to allow someone to create the conflict and then manipulate the department or administration into caving in such that the principles of the department are no longer being satisfied."

This might mean that the conflict will escalate, even to the point of going to court. "If the conflict was handled properly, and if the results can be supported, you shouldn't be afraid to go to court. You should not roll over under threat of a lawsuit. A good administrator should not let lawyers run the unit," Shedd says.

Strategies for Dealing with a Certified Jerk

Robert E. Cipriano

In a gentle way, you can shake the world.

—Mahatma Gandhi

Incivility and lack of collegiality are on the rise in institutions of higher education (Cipriano, 2011). This phenomenon can range from disputes and tension at one end of the spectrum to violence at the other. This fact unfortunately resonated in the extreme in January 2010 when Amy Bishop brought a nine-millimeter handgun to a faculty meeting and allegedly shot six fellow faculty members, killing three. There are many departments that suffer from non-collegial, uncivil, and nasty encounters between faculty members, faculty members and professional staff, and faculty members and students. Department chairs must deal with these types of encounters on a regular basis.

Many of us have seen how a toxic, uncivil, non-collegial faculty member can destroy a once-great department. Such a person can create an unhealthy and poisonous environment that deleteriously affects the entire department. Mean-spirited and uncivil people cause much damage to those they belittle, to the bystanders (students, staff, and department peers) who suffer the ripple effects, to the overall department performance, and to themselves. Faculty members who previously were stalwarts in the department simply disengage so that they are no longer targets to the malicious onslaught of nastiness perpetuated by this venomous person. A vicious cycle follows as faculty members retreat so they are not subject to this person's nasty attacks, students change majors because the climate in the department is contaminated, the chair becomes frustrated in her attempt to stop the escalating asperity, and the administration is swept up in the detritus of this department.

And in some cases, the provost and president declare fiscal emergency and the department is dissolved. This may seem an unlikely scenario, but it has happened in the past in more or less the same sequence.

Collegiality matters

Felps, Mitchell, and Byington (2006) wrote that having just one slacker or jerk in a group can bring down the team's overall performance by 30 to 40 percent. Stanford University professor Robert Sutton (2007) indicates that "having just a few nasty, lazy or incompetent characters around can ruin the performance of a team or an entire organization—no matter how stellar the other employees."

People throughout all institutions of higher education have indicated that collegiality is a subjective term that could be used to "get someone." Collegiality, reflected in the relationships that emerge within departments, has evoked a great deal of controversy throughout higher education. Without a consistent and well-defined sense of what constitutes collegiality, many chairs and deans resort to the dodge of "I recognize it when I see it," creating situations in which the likelihood of grievances, lawsuits, and increased department tension is extremely high. Cipriano and Buller have developed an instrument, called the Collegiality Assessment Matrix (CAM), that reflects those *observable behaviors* that are regarded as most highly related to the ways in which collegiality is demonstrated in an academic setting. The CAM, along with a slightly modified version for faculty members to complete (S-AM), were pilot-tested by chairs and faculty members. The chairs and faculty members who pilot-tested both matrices rated them as instruments that were highly useable, measured a person's observable collegial behaviors, and held great promise for use on an institution-wide basis.

There is little doubt or debate that lack of collegiality is a pressing problem throughout institutions of higher education. As part of their continuing research, Cipriano and Riccardi (2013, in press) conducted a national survey of chairs to begin to investigate how pervasive this phenomenon truly was. One of the questions that 528 chairs responded to was: "Have you ever had an uncivil or non-collegial faculty member in your department?" Eighty-eight chairs (N = 16.7 percent) responded "NO," and 440 (N = 83.3 percent) responded "YES."

We thought it would be interesting to determine strategies that chairs thought would work when dealing with a non-collegial faculty member. We mailed 1,700 surveys to chairs throughout the U.S. A total of 549 chairs responded, a 32.3 percent return rate. The survey had a total of 21 suggestions as to what a chair would do with a non-collegial faculty member, broken into four themes: positive, punitive, proactive, or just doing nothing. Positive items suggested approaches such as mentoring and legacy building, while proactive measures would take the support a step further, from having a one-on-one, forthright discussion with the individual to contacting appropriate upper-level administrators or human resources. Punitive options included more frequent teaching evaluations, unpopular course scheduling options, and more intense examination of the individual's sick/personal time.

Clearly, most department chairs understood that "wishing the problem away" was not a viable option, as only 11.7 percent would elect to "do nothing." The most popular approach was to have an open and frank discussion with the faculty member (92.8 percent), with almost four-fifths of the respondents preferring to have that discussion on campus (79.8 percent). Other highly favored proactive approaches were contacting the dean (80.3 percent), writing a letter to the individual explaining the problems (60.2 percent), and contacting the human resources department (57.0 percent). Similarly, a few positive suggestions yielded high results: asking what you as department chair could do to help (66.7 percent) and legacy building (51.9 percent). Most of the punitive recommendations scored below 5 percent, with only two in double digits: observing the individual's teaching in the classroom more frequently (17.8 percent) and not scheduling the individual for summer employment (15.7 percent).

Collegiality really matters

When over four-fifths of those surveyed affirm that they have had a non-collegial faculty member in their department, we have a problem. When one bad apple spoils a bunch, and we can universally identify that apple by name, we have a problem. When respondents write that their approach to dealing with that "bad apple" is to bury them under the grandstands behind the football field, we really have a problem. But when we support productive dissent, agreeing to disagree without being disagreeable, we have a solution. When we are clear and candid in our expectations of our colleagues, i.e., what is collegiality and what is not collegiality, we have a solution. When we use the CAM and the S-AM as a springboard to honest discussion about what constitutes collegiality in our academic work environment, we have a solution. So the question for all of us in the academy is simple: will we be part of the problem or part of the solution?

References

Cipriano, R. E. (2011). *Facilitating a collegial department in higher education: Strategies for success*. San Francisco: Jossey-Bass.

Felps, W., Mitchell, T. R., & Byington, E. (2006). How, when, and why bad apples spoil the barrel: Negative group members and dysfunctional groups. *Research in Organizational Behavior, 27*, 175–222. https://doi.org/10.1016/S0191-3085(06)27005-9

Sutton, R. I. (2007). *The no asshole rule: Building a civilized workforce and surviving one that isn't*. New York: Warner Business Books.

How to Respond to Toxic Leadership: Six Practical Approaches

Stephanie Hinshaw

Do you work for a dean, provost, president, or department chair who belittles you regularly? Or someone who seems to enjoy criticizing you and brings up your past mistakes? Perhaps your leader is someone who believes they are destined for greatness and refuses to admit they have faults. Or do you report to a leader who has explosive outbursts and unpredictable moods? Maybe none of these apply and the person you work for is simply trying to solve problems with other departments and has asked you to help "bring them down."

If any of these descriptions seems familiar, you may be working for a toxic leader. Toxic leaders are leaders who through a range of counterproductive to destructive behaviors leave organizations and followers worse than when they found them (Lipman-Blumen, 2005).

In today's global society, toxic leaders are entirely too common. Admittedly, I have no way to officially quantify the percentage of leaders who are toxic or the number of individuals who report to toxic leaders. But most people I have met when researching and discussing toxic leadership have shared that they reported to or are reporting to a toxic leader. Despite the high frequency of toxic leaders, we rarely discuss them, how they affect us, or how to respond to them.

If you find yourself in this unfortunate situation, the six strategies listed below may help you survive.

Attempt to coach the leader

In some cases, a leader may be unaware that their actions harm others or are inappropriate (Lipman-Blumen, 2005). Thus, I believe in giving them (and everyone) the benefit of the doubt in the beginning. In these instances, discuss your feelings with your leader and provide specific examples of their actions and the feelings they caused. If they seem genuinely receptive, provide them with some leadership resources (books, articles, videos, etc.). If they are not receptive, at least you know you tried and can move on to another approach. (I have found that I always feel better with other actions if I have attempted to address this problem directly first.)

Find support

Reporting to a toxic leader is hard and finding individuals who can support you through this experience is important. Talk with your family, friends, or mentors about what you are going through, and lean on them for guidance. The best support, however, can be found in colleagues who are experiencing the same toxic leader. Identifying an authentic collegial support system can help you feel less alone and confused. These colleagues are perfect for swapping stories, coping, and strategizing ways to address the situation or leader.

Use your voice

Followers of extremely toxic leaders often forget they have power. Often, they go to work and hear how little power they have from their leaders; thus, the followers start believing nothing can be done about their situation. This is rarely the case (Padilla, Hogan, & Kaiser, 2007). If you are in this situation, you can use your voice to elevate your concerns to your leader's manager, your president, human resources, your board, your accrediting agency, or other third parties. Remind yourself of your options, and use them when they feel right. Remember: when a toxic leader is exposed, we often ask why no one said anything before.

Create boundaries

Know that you are dealing with a toxic leader who probably does not recognize or respect boundaries. With this in mind, if you establish rules, you will more than likely end up in uncomfortable and bothersome situations. Spend time identifying your boundaries and then stick to them. If one of your boundaries is that you are unwilling to work on weekends, make sure you do not answer emails on weekends and refuse to make exceptions to this rule for something critical. Likewise, if one of your boundaries is avoiding conversations that put down others, excuse yourself from those conversations when they start or change the subject. You have more control than you think, and it all starts with setting your boundaries and not budging on them then sticking to them—no matter what.

Protect your character and integrity

Much like creating boundaries, you can protect your integrity by knowing your limits and values. In other words, you do not have to stoop to your leader's level. When your leader is angry, you can be calm. When they are disrespectful, you can be kind. While behaving this way is sometimes hard in the moment, it helps you feel better when you look at yourself in the mirror and ask whether you like what you see (trust me on this one).

Be kind to yourself

The kindness mentioned above should apply not only to others but also to you. Acknowledge that you are in a difficult situation, and allow yourself to feel hurt, disappointed, and confused. Give yourself time to process these feelings, and do not discount them because "it's just work." Work, our work lives, and our work relationships are important to us and matter. So treat the situation as if you were going through a difficult time with a friend or family member and do what helps you feel better. That may be meditating, working out, reading, traveling, spending time with loved ones, or finding a new position. Whatever it is, make sure to take care of yourself.

These are just six possible ways to respond to toxic leaders. Hopefully at least one approach here can assist you. It is also important to know that you are not alone, others have gone through this and survived, and you should handle the situation in whatever way that feels best for you. Much like protecting your character, you must decide what you're willing to live with as you approach this situation.

References

Lipman-Blumen, J. (2005). *The allure of toxic leaders*. Oxford, England: Oxford University Press.

Padilla, A., Hogan, R., & Kaiser, R. B. (2007). The toxic triangle: Destructive leaders, susceptible followers, and conducive environments. *The Leadership Quarterly, 18*(3), 176–194. https://doi.org/10.1016/j.leaqua.2007.03.001

Developing Critical Cross-cultural Communicative Competence in Academic Leaders

Abdelilah Salim Sehlaoui

According to Chun and Evans (2018), continued white hegemonic practices in university and college administration and faculty have failed to develop a representative institutional culture and organizational structure that is responsive to the needs of diverse students and faculty. The purpose of this article is to discuss this issue, relate it to how the concept of culture is used in education from a critical perspective, and share with you a set of recommendations, activities, and strategies based on not only on research, but my direct personal experience as a minority faculty member and academic leader, and my interactions with other faculty and students who are culturally and linguistically diverse.

My recommendations and analysis of this issue are based on the fundamental concept of culture that is at the heart of what we do as human beings. The term culture is defined here within its socioeconomic and political context and as part of such a context. It is viewed as a dynamic process in which individuals are in a constant struggle for representation and the need to have an authentic voice (e.g. Sehlaoui, 1999, 2011, 2018a; Giroux, 1992; Quantz, 1992). Figure 1 illustrates the fundamental role this critical view of culture plays and the interactive and dynamic relationship that exists between three complex competences with a focus on the *critical cross-cultural communicative competence* (C5) that is more relevant to our discussion of diversity and inclusion.

According to Sehlaoui (1999, 2011, 2018b), C5 is defined as our ability to effectively communicate across cultures and with diverse individuals, to create a *representative* administration that is *responsive to the needs of diverse students and faculty*. C^5 involves respect, tolerance, and critical understanding of various points of view while allowing culturally and linguistically diverse individuals to share power relations and have an authentic voice (Sehlaoui, 2011). It's a view of a transformational leadership that empowers others.

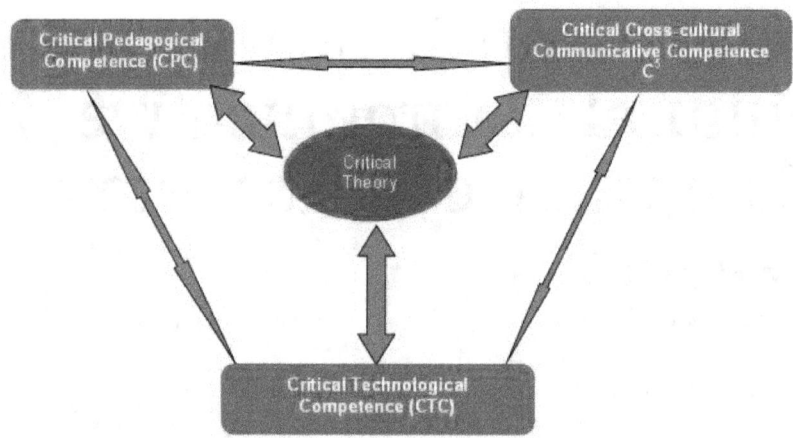

Figure 1. C5, CPC, and CTC: A Dialectical Interactive Relationship
Source: Sehlaoui, 2011, 2018

Both systemic and individual factors contribute to our problematic situation. For example, Chun and Evans (2018), among others, document the facts that

- over the past decade many racist incidents have occurred at colleges and universities;
- the hostile and divisive national political climate poses an obstacle to creating representative and culturally responsive higher education institutions today; and
- diversity is often used as a marketing tool to showcase an institution in a positive light rather than given priority and incorporated in a systemic manner to become part of the institutions' strategic plan.

At the systemic level, even when a minority faculty member has the ability to lead and possesses the qualities identified by researchers as it relates to leadership and success, the presence of stereotypes, racism, and biases often prevail over positive leadership characteristics that a minority individual holds (Chun & Evans, 2018; Gordon, 2000). This observation was corroborated to me as minority faculty and as an academic leader during my

32 years of experience in the field of education and through my interactions with other minority individuals who have made similar observations. Research has addressed these issues at the systemic level and the following is a brief description of some of the suggested strategies and recommendations.

Research-based recommendations for bringing change

Chun and Evans (2018) stress the need for a new leadership model "to reshape and replace hierarchical and elite modes of governance and build inclusive environments for diverse faculty, staff, administrators, and students" (p. 221). Other researchers also stress the need for bold and courageous leadership to overcome internal and external forces resisting diversity change (Allen, 2018; Clark, Fasching-Varner, & Brimhall-Vargas, 2012).

Internal forces, according to Chun and Evans (2018), are created by what they describe as "continued dominance of white, male, heterosexual perspectives in university and college administration" (p. xiii). To overcome these hegemonic internal practices, these researchers, among others, call for the importance of devoting significant funding resources to diversity and inclusion initiatives and practices. They also emphasize new diverse and dynamic models of leadership that use strategies that aim at

- building teamwork;
- valuing cultural differences;
- creating *trust-based* rather than *fear-based* environments; and
- using an administration system that is *culturally responsive, representative*, and *powerful enough* to bring about organizational change.

Of course, as is the case with any challenge or problem, the first step is to recognize or identify the problem. The following statement was shared with me by a colleague at a state university: "I think our college is on target with diversity and inclusion. I don't see any problem in that area. We invite culturally diverse individuals to apply for our faculty positions and we hire them. We also reach out to diverse student populations. We have a good percentage of diverse students and faculty."

Statements like these illustrate a denial stage in the process of developing an authentic critical cross-cultural communication dialogue (Sehlaoui, 2011). As a result, institutions of higher education need to offer their academic leaders professional development opportunities to develop their C^5. Many researchers have identified key features of successful diversity organizational learning programs. For example, Chun and Evans (2018) shared 20 strategies and recommendations based on their research. Other recommended research-based and system-related strategies include the following:

- Offering classes in cross-cultural communication competencies at the

graduate and undergraduate levels and measuring impact after completion/graduation (Sehlaoui, 2011; 2018a). These courses focus on the critical view of cultural dynamics and move beyond the positivist, hegemonic, and traditional views of education.
- Creating centers for advocacy for critical cross-cultural and multicultural education and supporting them financially (Chun & Evans, 2018).
- Providing incentives for faculty and staff to seek training in organizational diversity and inclusion to develop their C^5 (Wilson, 2018).
- Creating mentoring and supportive programs to encourage faculty from minority groups to hold decision-making positions and build structures of support to retain them (Norhafezah, Rosna, Nena, & Aizan, 2018). It is not enough to hire a minority person to serve in a leadership position when the climate in such an institution may not be welcoming or supportive of diversity and inclusion.
- Finally, institutions of higher education should also support and engage their academic leaders in opportunities to genuinely engage in global educational programs, especially since our world is becoming more and more diverse.

Projected US demographics

While there is need for systematic organizational learning to implement diversity culture change across campus (Chun & Evans, 2018; Saathoff, 2017), it should be noted that cultural change is a gradual process that is influenced by our nation's ever-changing demographics (Stanley, Watson, Reyes, & Varela, 2018). According to Goldstein (2016), "census projections show that by the 2050 Census, the United States will no longer have a clear white majority—at least as we define 'white' today. Fifty-three percent of the population will be multiracial or nonwhite, compared with less than 40% currently."

Researchers believe this racial shift will happen even if the federal government issues new restrictive immigration policies, because the growth of the nonwhite population is driven more by fertility than by immigration. These demographic changes are a reality and institutions of higher education need to adapt and be prepared to face the challenge by providing diverse and inclusive leadership styles and institutional cultures.

Promoting change: a critical incident process-oriented approach

Thus far we have looked at the lack of diversity and inclusion initiatives and practices in higher education from the systemic level; let us now consider it from the individual level and provide some recommendations for addressing the problem.

At the individual level, researchers in multilingual and multicultural education (e.g., Grant & Sleeter, 2011; Sehlaoui 1999, 2001, 2018a, 2018b), and others in the area of leadership as it relates to the issue of diversity and inclusion (e.g. Chun & Evans, 2018), have identified a number of key challenges:

- Power struggles where the more powerful people impose their agendas and interests on the less powerful
- Lack of critical cross-cultural communicative competence among educators and academic leaders results in more conflicts that perpetuate the status quo
- Ignorance breeds more fear and anxiety
- Lack of representation in curriculum and instruction as well as leadership leads to educational failure of individuals and financial losses for societies

From this critical perspective, culture is seen as a site of struggle, a place where multiple interpretations come together but where there is always a dominant force based on asymmetrical power relations that exist in each socio-economic and political context. Higher education institutions are examples of these contexts. Figure 2 illustrates that at the individual level, people tend to focus on the tip of the iceberg, which covers the physical traits and superficial facts and numbers/stats that may be misleading when it comes to issues of diversity and inclusion and the development of C^5. The hidden part of the iceberg is what usually counts the most in terms of representation of diverse individuals in the power dynamics and decision-making processes of an institution.

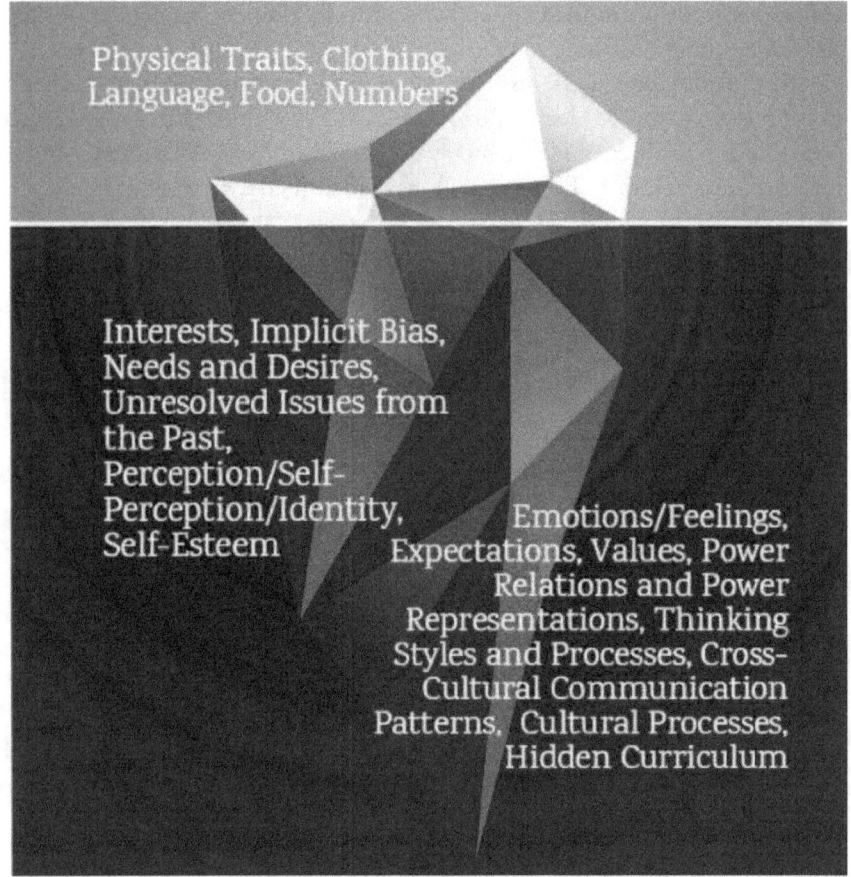

Figure 2. The Diversity and Inclusion Iceberg Analogy

Critical theorists and pedagogues conclude that cross-cultural communication, including computer-mediated communication, cannot be understood without considering the power dynamics of relationships (Sehlaoui, 2011, 2018a). Understanding the power dynamics of a situation cannot be achieved in isolation. The dynamic nature of the concept of cultural identity is in an interactional relationship with the concepts of power, communication, context, and culture, with the latter concept being at the center of these interactional and dialectical relationships (see Figure 3).

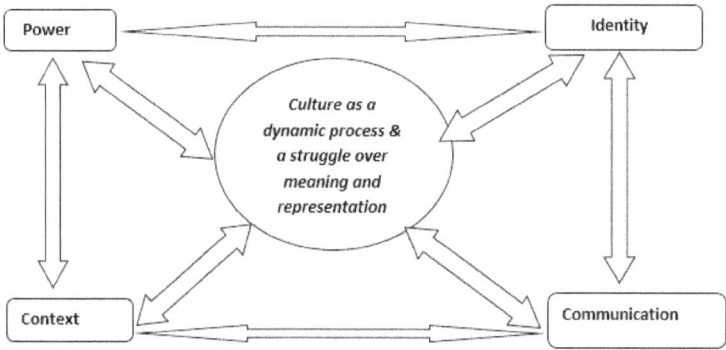

Figure 3. Culture, Power, Context, Identity, and Communication:
A Dialectical Interrelationship.
Source: Adapted from Sehlaoui (2011)

Professional development activities that aim to address the issue of diversity and inclusion at the individual level should be based on a critical definition of culture and the processes involved in the development of C^5 in key leadership personnel (Sehlaoui, 2018a, 2018b). The critical pedagogical approach advocated in this article recommends use of critical-incident professional development activities during which participants are faced with scenarios and situations where issues of diversity and inclusion are focused on from various viewpoints. Activities such as the following can be adapted from Sehlaoui (1999 and 2018b):

- Cross-cultural dialogues
- Case studies, critical incidents, and scenarios
- Matching exercise: The Stages of C^5 Continuum

However, it should be emphasized that prior to engaging in such professional development activities, faculty and leaders must (1) recognize that there is a problem, (2) define the problem, (3) create a non-threatening climate for an authentic cross-cultural dialogue to take place, and (4) develop what Chun and Evans (2018) call "a sustained and deliberate institutional planning and action" (p. xvi).

Cross-cultural dialogue activity: In this activity, participants are invited to explore some cultural processes and patterns of communication, such as polychronic vs. mono-chronic (see this article: https://doi.org/10.1002/9781118783665.ieicc0110), the process of stereotyping, and implicit bias, by having them act out the cross-cultural dialogues and discuss the cross-cultural communication issues that may contribute to reinforcing hegemonic practices at the individual level.

Case studies/critical incident/scenarios: In this activity, participants are invited to explore cases of implicit institutional bias and hegemonic practices while exploring the concept of hidden curriculum. The hidden curriculum is defined in critical pedagogy as being an implicit curriculum. Rather than coming about by design, it represents behaviors, attitudes, and knowledge that are communicated without conscious intent—it is an accumulation of values communicated indirectly, through actions and words that are part of everyday life in a community (Giroux, 1981 and 1992). Because it is hidden, it requires more attention and direct observation in educational settings. Participants in these exercises should study the concepts of hidden curriculum and implicit bias and share effective strategies on how to address them within their unique institutional context.

Matching exercise to assess the stages of C^5 continuum: This assessment activity is adapted from Bennett's (1993) ethno-relativist model. Participants are provided with statements related to diversity and inclusion that were anonymously collected from individuals. Based on these statements, participants work together to match the statements with the stages of the C^5. The purpose is to raise awareness of these stages of development so as to create inclusive and culturally responsive leadership practices.

The goal of activities such as these is to develop in the participants the language of critique and the language of possibility. According to Giroux (1981), the language of critique is defined as the participants' ability to defend their pedagogical decisions/practices in front of various audiences. It also refers to their ability to discover the hidden curriculum and to define, recognize, and document the existence of issues of diversity and inclusion in their institutions in a proactive way.

Qualitative methods of measuring diversity and inclusion progress

When it comes to assessing the progress being made in the area of diversity and inclusion in higher education, according to research (e.g. Chun & Evans, 2018; Taylor, Beck, Lahey & Froyd, 2017; Wolff et al., 2015), numbers and percentages of representation alone are meaningless unless we focus on *measures of influence and power*. For example, at any given institution, we should measure:

- Minority individuals' titles and level within an institution of higher education to show how much relative power they have.
- How often minority individuals attend pivotal meetings and councils, or how much they are involved in key decision-making processes.

- Other guiding questions in measuring diversity and inclusion practices may include:
- Who's invited to a meeting or to participate in research, grant projects, committees? Who gets to speak and how often? Are we leaving out anyone whose input would be valuable?
- Have we created conditions where every person can contribute in their unique and meaningful way while feeling safe and secure by doing so? If not, do we have the courage to admit there is a problem and work together to change it?
- How much money do we invest in addressing issues of diversity and inclusion?
- Are we aware of how the norms, power structures, and inequities in society can easily become embedded in an institution? If so, what have we done about it?

These are just some examples of the types of questions that can be posed when trying to assess diversity and inclusion at our institutions. Because each institution is unique, the questions used to effectively guide the assessment process will vary.

Conclusion

I will close this article with a slide from my presentation at the 2018 Leadership in Higher Education Conference. It illustrates necessary components for promoting culturally responsive campuses. To achieve this goal, institutions of higher education need to use both top-down and bottom-up processes and strategies for organizational cultural change that are based on trust, sustained efforts, moral and financial support, and the creation of a positive and safe environment. The need for continuous professional development and networking at the individual and institutional levels is necessary to facilitate and support such a change. Ongoing assessment of the effectiveness of the diversity and inclusion plan is cyclical in this model.

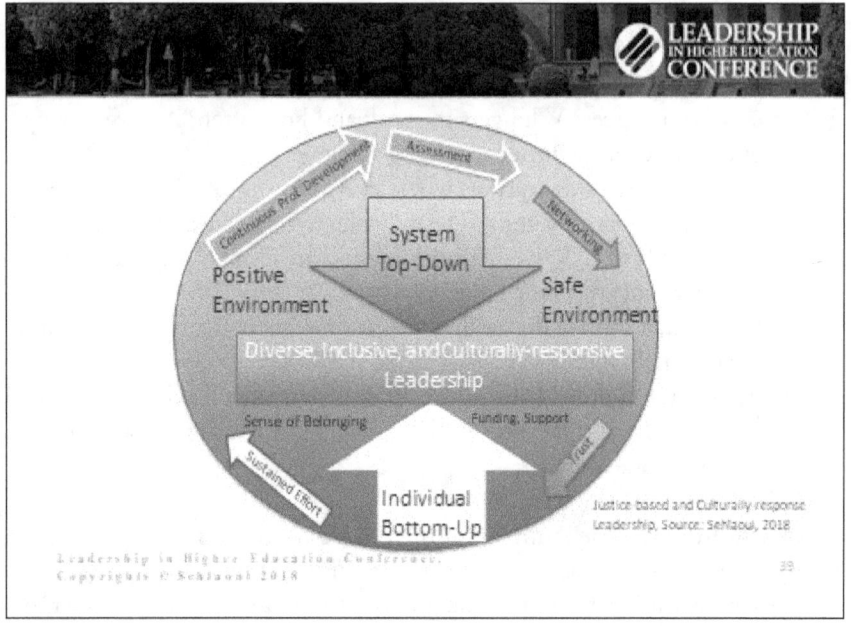

References

Allen, S. (2018). Creative diversity: Promoting interculturality in Australian pathways to higher education. *Journal of International Students, 8*(1), 251–273.

Bennett, M. J. (1993). Towards ethnorelativism: A developmental model of intercultural sensitivity. In R. M. Paige (Ed.), *Education for the intercultural experience*. Yarmouth, ME: Intercultural Press.

Chun, E., & Evans, A. (2018). *Leading a diversity culture shift in higher education: Comprehensive organizational learning strategies.* New York, NY: Routledge.

Clark, C., Fasching-Varner, K. J., & Brimhall-Vargas, M. (2012). *Occupying the academy: Just how important is diversity work in higher education?* Rowman & Littlefield.

Giroux, H. A. (1981). *Ideology, culture and the process of schooling.* Barcombe, England: Falmer Press.

Giroux, H. (1992). Critical literacy and student experience: Donald Graves' approach to literacy. In P. Shannon (Ed.), *Becoming political: Readings and writings in the politics of education*. Portsmouth, NH: Heinemann.

Goldstein, D. (2016). America: This is your future. Retrieved from https://www.politico.com/agenda/story/2016/11/political-future-of-america-generations-diversity-tensions-000235

Grant, C. & Sleeter, C. E. (2011). *Doing multicultural education for achievement and equity.* New York, NY: Routledge.

Norhafezah, Y., Rosna A. H., Nena P. V., & Aizan, Y. (2018). Managing diversity in higher education: A strategic communication approach. *Journal of Asian Pacific Communication, 28*(1), 41–60.

Quantz, R. A. (1992). On critical ethnography (with some postmodern considerations). In M. D. LeCompte, W. L. Millroy, and J. Preissle (Eds.), The handbook of qualitative research in education. San Diego, CA: Academic Press.

Saathoff, S. D. (2017). Healing systemic fragmentation in education through multicultural education. *Multicultural Education, 25*(1), 2–8.

Sehlaoui, A. S. (2001). Developing cross-cultural communicative competence in preservice ESL/EFL teachers: A critical perspective. *Language, Culture, and Curriculum Journal, 14*(1).

Sehlaoui, A. S. (1999). Developing cross-cultural communicative competence in ESL/EFL preservice teachers: A critical perspective. (Doctoral dissertation, Indiana University of Pennsylvania, 1999). *Dissertation Abstracts International, DAI-A 60/06,* p. 2042, Publication # 99348338.

Sehlaoui, A. S. (2011). *Developing ESL/EFL teachers' cross-cultural communicative competence: A research-based critical pedagogical model.* New York, NY: Lambert Academic Publishing.

Sehlaoui, A. S. (2018a). Teaching ESL and STEM content through CALLT: A research-based interdisciplinary critical pedagogical approach. Lanham, MD: Rowman & Littlefield.

Sehlaoui, A. S. (2018b). Critical cross-cultural communicative competence for academic leaders. Paper presented at the Leadership in Higher Education Conference, October 18–20, 2018, Minneapolis, MN.

Stanley, C. A., Watson, K. L., Reyes, J. M., & Varela, K. S. (2018). Organizational change and the chief diversity officer: A case study of institutionalizing a diversity plan. *Journal of Diversity in Higher Education.* Retrieved from http://dx.doi.org/10.1037/dhe0000099

Taylor, L. L., Beck, M. I., Lahey, J. N., & Froyd, J. E. (2017). Reducing inequality in higher education: The link between faculty empowerment and climate and retention. *Innovative Higher Education, 42*(5-6), 391–405.

Wilson, J. L. (2018). A framework for planning organizational diversity: Applying multicultural practice in higher education work settings. *Planning for Higher Education, 46*(3), 23–32.

Wolff, J., Mills, C., Fricker, M., Putnam, D., Williams, B., Angier, T., Allais, L., Metz, T., Bilchitz, D., Glaser, D., & Cudd, A. E. (2015). *The equal society: Essays on equality in theory and practice.* Lexington Books.

Campus Incivility and Free Speech: A Contemporary Dilemma

Robert E. Cipriano and Jeffrey L. Buller

> *"Laws alone cannot secure freedom of expression; in order that every man present his views without penalty there must be a spirit of tolerance in the entire population. Such an ideal of external liberty can never be fully attained but must be sought unremittingly if scientific thought, and philosophical and creative thinking in general are to be advanced as far as possible."*
>
> —Albert Einstein (1950, p. 13)

Imagine this scenario. Dr. Upton O. Goode, chair of the Department of Organic Astral Therapy at Dicey Incline State University (DISU), has invited Ms. Stuckin D'Past, the founder of a group that's widely perceived as advocating white nationalism, to deliver a campus address on current challenges facing society. Dr. Goode has required all students majoring in organic astral therapy to attend, opened his own courses to Ms. D'Past for further discussion, and invited all other students to attend the public lecture.

The title that Ms. D'Past has chosen for her speech, "The Crime of Diversity," has attracted concern from students, faculty, and administrators alike. A large majority of those on campus believe that the speech will support the agenda for white nationalism and encourage violence. The League of Students for Diversity (LSD) has planned a massive protest at the event and reached out to DISU students, employees, and members of the community to join them. LSD has stated in emails that it intends to disrupt the event—by any and all means possible—to stop Ms. D'Past from speaking.

Mr. Barry D. Hatchett, the president of DISU, is afraid that if the speech is allowed to proceed, violence will erupt that his campus's security service will be unable to contain. The rhetoric around Ms. D'Past's appearance has so become strident that the local mayor and town council believe public safety may be at risk. Several outside groups, both supportive of and opposed to Ms. D'Past's group, have threatened to appear at the public event and advocate for their causes. President Hatchett is on the verge of canceling the presentation entirely when he receives an email from Dr. Goode indicating that any attempt by the administration to block Ms. D'Past from speaking would be regarded as violating the First Amendment and its guarantees of free speech as well as Dr. Goode's own academic freedom.

An official statement by Ms. D'Past said that she hoped all "right thinking" members of the community would come to the event and demonstrate their support of her right to speak and opposition to the "fascist tactics" of groups like LSD. Hearing the responses to this statement from listeners to call-in radio, Mr. Hatchett becomes even more concerned about what might happen at the public event.

President Hatchett knows that he must act quickly since the day of Ms. D'Past's arrival is rapidly approaching. He calls his cabinet into a joint session with his governing board and tries to work out a plan for how to proceed. The group makes the following accommodations. DISU will

- budget an additional $250,000 (taken from funds originally set aside for staff bonuses) for police to attend and monitor the public event and do what they can to prevent violence;
- offer Ms. D'Past a "safe space" to deliver her presentation;
- publicize the fact that the First Amendment does not provide anyone with the right to disrupt campus activities;
- establish bias response teams (BRTs) to monitor this event and similar activities in the future that have the potential for resulting in violence; and
- take a public stance that freedom of speech allows people to state their opinions without interference, retaliation, or punishment from the government.

Questions
1. What is your opinion of this proposed solution?
2. What would you do if you were the following people?
   a. President Hatchett
   b. Dr. Goode

c. The president of DISU's faculty senate

d. The president of the LSD

e. The chair of the governing board

f. The director of campus safety at DISU

g. The mayor of the city where DISU is located

h. The chief of police of the city where DISU is located

Background

We'll suggest a few possible answers to these questions, but first let's look at some background for our hypothetical case study. What is now known as the Free Speech Movement (FSM) began in 1964 as a series of protests at the University of California, Berkeley. These protests reached their climax on December 2, 1964, when, after a rally featuring the folk singer and activist Joan Baez, students occupied the administration building. This sit-in led to the arrest of 773 people. Many faculty members at the university supported the students and provided them with bail money. Clark Kerr, president of the University of California during these protests, refused to expel the student activists, arguing, "The University is not engaged in making ideas safe for students. It is engaged in making students safe for ideas. Thus it permits the freest expression of views before students, trusting to their good sense in passing judgment on these views. Only in this way can it best serve American democracy" (Berdahl, 2004). Kerr was fired three weeks after Ronald Reagan took office as the governor of California.

The issue of free speech on college and university campuses is as old as education itself and as current as today's news. Institutions of higher education often find themselves torn between their desire to create environments where students and professors remain physically safe and their mission to protect academic freedom and the right of free speech. What can academic leaders do to increase the likelihood that constructive conflicts between ideas don't escalate into destructive, violent acts?

Hate speech

One place to begin is with an understanding of what hate speech is and what it isn't. Some people use the expression *hate speech* to label any ideas they find difficult, troubling, controversial, or offensive. But **there is no such thing as a right, either constitutional or academic, not to be offended.** Legally, *hate speech* refers to expressions that insult or demean a person or a group of people on the basis of such attributes as race, religion, ethnic origin, sexual orientation, disability, and gender. But hate speech is not required to be speech per se. Nonverbal symbols may also be used to express hatred. For example, although the United States Supreme Court has ruled that burning the American flag (*Texas v. Johnson*, 491 U.S. 397 1989) and wearing armbands as an act of protest (*Tinker v. Des Moines Independent Community School District*, 393 U.S. 503 1969) are examples of protected speech, destruction of private property or the use of these same nonverbal symbols to threaten someone is not. As a result, painting a swastika on the interior wall of your home library is permitted, but painting a swastika on the wall of your public library is not. Free speech also does not protect those who engage in defamation of character, child pornography, harassment, invasion of privacy, and other types of expression already restricted by law. In addition, colleges and universities retain the right to establish the *time*, *place*, and *manner* in which protests or other potentially disruptive expressions of free speech may occur.

In US law, hate speech is not regarded as a separate category of speech. Whether one likes it or not, most hate speech is protected under the First Amendment as a variety of "unpopular speech." A number of countries (including Germany) do have laws prohibiting incitement to racial or ethnic hatred, but the United States isn't one of them. The rationale for protecting unpopular speech is that there is simply no practical way to regulate hate speech without censoring ideas, and censoring ideas should be particularly offensive to everyone, especially those who work in higher education. Gresham's Law in economics states that "bad money drives out good." But a type of Reverse Gresham's Law applies to higher education: good ideas drive out bad ideas. As the Supreme Court Justice Louis D. Brandeis established in the case of *Whitney v. California*, "If there be time to expose through discussion, the falsehoods and fallacies, to avert the evil by the processes of education, the remedy to be applied is more speech, not enforced silence" (*Whitney v. California*, 274 U.S. 357 1927). In other words, the solution to "bad speech" is not less speech but more.

It is important to remember, too, that in the United States, speech protections under the First Amendment apply only to governmental speech. So the law works differently for public than it does for private universities. A religious college or seminar is legally entitled to restrict what is said or taught on its campus. But if a private school advertises itself as an environment that is open to all ideas or where opinions may be freely exchanged, it has then provided a *contractual obligation* to permit free speech. So if someone violates the right of free speech at a public university, it could become a federal matter. If, on the other hand, someone violates the right of free speech at a private university, it could become a civil matter. The university is sued, not prosecuted. (See, for example, "First Amendment on Private Campuses," 2015, and Dynia & Hudson, 2017.)

Conclusions

Readers will undoubtedly have their own ideas about how they would handle the hypothetical situation at DISU. We all approach challenges differently, based on our own experience and the traditions at our universities. But here is one possible way of proceeding. First, it's important to identify where the central issue in this case study lies. People merely *believe* that Ms. D'Past's speech will support the agenda for white nationalism and encourage violence, but the LSD has explicitly *threatened* in emails that it intends to disrupt the event by any and all means possible. Canceling the public event would thus involve *prior restraint* of free speech, which is illegal, but LSD's documented incitement of others to violence or lawless action is *not* protected free speech and may suitably be investigated by the police.

Second, while President Hatchett is suitably concerned about the safety of his faculty and students, many of the solutions proposed by his cabinet and governing board take only a *short-term approach*. With the exception of creating Bias Response Teams (themselves questionable since they appear to be designed for prior restraint of free speech), none of the proposed actions involve substantive, *long-term approaches*. DISU should also consider developing publications or web pages that explain what free speech is, what "time, place, and manner" restrictions are, and how the institution will both protect free speech and address expressions that are deemed threats or incitements to violence. In other words, DISU should make this challenge a teachable moment. A good example of an institution that has created this type of website is North Carolina State University (Free Speech, 2020).

Third, President Hatchett should consider launching a program that educates students—as well as faculty members and administrators—on how differences of opinion can be expressed *constructively* and how to discuss sensitive or contentious issues. Excellent examples of this approach are Widener University's Common Ground Initiative (Common Ground, n.d.), the University of Alaska at Anchorage's programs Start Talking (Landis, 2008) and Toxic Friday (Roderick, 2016), and Florida Atlantic University's Agora Project (The FAU Agora Project, n.d.).

Free speech on college and university campuses will continue to present significant challenges to academic leaders. As with so many of today's issues, there is no "one size fits all" strategy that can bring about a perfect accommodation between campus civility and free speech. Addressing the challenges we all face as academic leaders will require a great deal of effort, compromise, and mutual understanding on the part of students, faculty members, and administrators alike if we want to promote truly free scholarly inquiry while simultaneously creating a culture of respect for those who oppose other people's ideas.

References

Berdahl, R. M. (2004). *Clark Kerr memorial.* Retrieved from https://chancellor.berkeley.edu/chancellors/berdahl/speeches/clark-kerr-memorial

Common Ground: Widener University. (n.d.) Retrieved from https://www.widener.edu/about/points-pride/common-ground

Dynia, P. A., & Hudson, D. L. (2017, September). Rights of students. *The First Amendment Encyclopedia.* Retrieved from https://mtsu.edu/first-amendment/article/931/rights-of-students

Einstein, A. (1950). *Albert Einstein: Out of my later years.* New York, NY: Philosophical Library.

The FAU Agora Project: Florida Atlantic University. (n.d.) Retrieved from http://www.fau.edu/agora

First Amendment on private campuses. (2015, December 1). *Harvard Civil Rights-Civil Liberties Law Review.* Retrieved from https://harvardcrcl.org/first-amendment-on-private-campuses

Free Speech: North Carolina State University. Retrieved from https://www.ncsu.edu/free-speech

Landis, K. (Ed.) (2008). *Start talking: A handbook for engaging difficult dialogues in higher education.* Anchorage, AK: The University of Alaska Anchorage and Alaska Pacific University.

Roderick, L. (Ed.) (2016). *Toxic Friday: Resources for addressing faculty bullying in higher education.* Anchorage, AK: The University of Alaska Anchorage.

PART III

Leading Through Change

How to Lead Change from the Middle

Jon M. Garon

When I focus on managing change, I often emphasize the writings of Peter Drucker. A nationally recognized expert on organizational change in the noneducation setting, Drucker focused on seven stressors that typically are responsible for most changes to organizations. These find their place in higher education just as they did throughout industry.

Generally, the stressors Drucker identified fall into two broad categories. On the one hand, there are external changes, such as demographic shifts; shifts in population; new knowledge (whether scientific or nonscientific); and changes in the perception, mood, and meaning of the world around us. On the other, there are internal changes. Here, we look at the unexpected: unexpected lessons, successes, and failures. We look at incongruities, the difference between how things actually are and how they ought to be. We look at innovation based on process change, and we look at changes in industry structure, market structure, or other externalities within the industry that catch everybody unaware.

Externally, demographic shifts are coming to higher education. We see tremendous change right now. We see a significant change in the birth rates in the United States. We see significant shifts in social change pertaining to gender, race, and ethnicity as well as who's going to college and why. We see economic shifts with rising college costs and the movement for free college tuition. The pricing model is also under tremendous pressure at the moment. We find weaknesses in employment for some categories, such as the PhD and JD. We see changing in student preparedness coming out of the K–12 system. And we see a shift in the role of international students as part of our population and as part of our economic models.

New knowledge, of course, is always changing higher education. We're also seeing new knowledge about the way we teach with new tools, such as e-learning, online and flipped classrooms, and the emphasis on experiential learning. We also see a great unknown: the growth of artificial intelligence, which could significantly change many of our processes and many of the ways we do things. In short, external change is truly sweeping through higher education.

Internally, we see in the category of perception, mood, and meaning that quite a bit has changed with the role the university plays for its students and community. We see demands for housing, medical services, food services, and community resources. We see a shift toward more and more brand recognition of fewer and fewer universities. We see increasing regulations and compliance obligations, such as Title IX, Title IV, ADA, and other regulatory models. And finally there's social media, which is changing the communications around the university and, as a result, changing how we control our brand message and how we communicate with students, faculty, alumni, and donors.

With all these changes, what do we as deans and department chairs do to handle this transformation? Well, it starts with the vision of the university. But the role of creating and developing the university vision is really that of the president and the board of trustees. Although we chairs and deans are not responsible for crafting the university-wide mission, it is our responsibility to ensure that the vision can be lived out in our programs and departments and is grounded in research, in science, and in the important aspects of what we do within our institution.

So how do we do that? First, we must make sure that the programs we operate align strategically with that vision. We can do this by identifying key structures within those programs and tying them directly to that vision statement. Second, as the chief communication officers within our communities, we need to be working with our stakeholders—our chairs, faculty members, students, and alumni—to make sure that we're consistent with the messaging as to what we do and why we do it and how that fits tightly into the vision of the university. Third, we know that unit-level change tends to be much nimbler than university-wide change. And so, we can look within our organizations to see where we can effect positive change to make sure we address the stressors discussed above.

Remember that disruption requires breathing space. We have seen across industry that one of the best ways to develop strategic change is through a skunkworks module. This approach involves taking a small group out of their traditional roles, giving them some autonomy, and quite frankly allowing them to fail if in fact their experiments don't work. When we operate exclusively within structure, it becomes much harder for teams to be effective. It raises the stakes for what we're trying to accomplish. But when we work with small teams that are on the margins, they can become more experimental, and the learning from those teams can then be brought back into our basic structures. That way there's synergy between the skunkworks ideation and the ongoing operations of the institution. One doesn't want to do everything as a one-off, because then there's no trust, no sense of rigor, and no sense of consistency. But when everything is done through a slow, stilted process, it's unlikely that the organization will have the nimbleness necessary for it to effect new change.

Remember that most disruptors fail. That's just fine. One of the biggest mistakes that organizations can make is thinking that every innovation strategy is going to be a success strategy. Historically, most attempts at innovation, most new businesses, most projects, simply fail. If they're designed to make failure an acceptable option, the organizations can move on very easily. It's only when the success or failure of an innovation becomes do or die for the organization that the stakes become too high and it becomes ineffective. So, create teams that are allowed to experiment. If the answer of the experiment is "we shouldn't do this," then that's an acceptable outcome. If the answer is "we tried this, we had a small sample size, and what we learned was we're not very good at this," that's OK too. Learning to fail is perfectly acceptable and part of the development strategy in every for-profit sector, and it's essential it becomes integral into the nonprofit and educational sectors as well.

Remember that disruption is inevitable. The organization needs to plan accordingly for the disruption that we know is going to happen. The best way to start to deal with the inevitability of disruption is to have a team and a group of stakeholders that are prepared for the coming disruption, even if it's not clear what that disruption will be. What that means is that we work with our management teams to make sure they're prepared to handle the disruption. We do that by selecting team members who have the nimbleness and vision to address unknown challenges. We make sure that we've trained our teams. We make sure we've run through thought exercises that allow team members to feel comfortable in an insecure and changing environment. And we work with all of our stakeholders—our donor community, our peer deans and department chairs, our students, and our alumni—to ensure that everybody involved understands the kind of changes that we're looking at and where we fit into this changing landscape.

Now, the number one way to address changes is clearly with resources. But often in this environment, we don't have additional funds. We don't have free resources to allocate, particularly to efforts that may fail. So we have to again focus on nimbleness and scaling our responses to make sure we have proof of concept before we deal with a given change. By working with strong teams and communicating with our stakeholders, we can make sure that everybody understands that change is coming and how we'll address it—even if we don't know exactly what the change will be.

So how do we as deans and chairs specifically embrace these changes? I have four suggestions.

- **Embrace the role of the dean.** Again, deans are middle management. We can't assume the role of the presidents or the board of trustees. Instead, we need to understand that we are there to facilitate communication—a conversation between the senior leadership on one side and students, faculty, and alumni on the other. That way we can make sure we're delivering a high-quality education, that we're getting the student outcomes that we desire, and that the vision is congruent with the needs of our students and our community.
- **Find your place in the middle.** That means working on self-awareness, agility, systematic thinking, communication agility, and influence. Use the tools that come to us as deans—as thought leaders, coaches, mentors, and partners with our students, faculty, and staff—to build a relationship. Challenging changes are much harder if there's no trust. If you can build trust and create a shared sense of responsibility, then it will be much easier for you to work together to effect change.
- **Accept the complexity you're faced with.** There are no simple answers to the changes that are coming to higher education. And anyone who thinks that they can sloganize this, turn it into simple, quick answers, is going to be deeply challenged and surprised by the complexities they face. But if you share those complexities in a positive way and explain that although you're facing complex, wicked problems, you have a shared responsibility to address them and the resilience to get through them, then you can build a community that can address those challenges as you go forward.
- **Retain your passion for what makes higher education so important.** Again, most of us are here because of the teaching to make sure our students are successful. Most of us are here because of the primary research to make sure we're actually bringing new knowledge into the world, disseminating that knowledge for the public. That core mission, that fundamental, has not changed.

The externalities and process changes are simply steps toward those two primary goals. If we stay focused on those two goals, then everything else will fall into place. That does not mean that they're not complex, wicked problems. It means that they fit into a much more important context of learning outcomes for our students, new knowledge, and new research for society.

Finally, here are a few suggestions on how deans can lead through these disruptions.

- **Command the bully pulpit.** As the dean, you have access to a significant number of opportunities to communicate with the public. Using that opportunity is essential. And you should use the bully pulpit to embrace the complexity of the situation you're facing. Rather than simplifying your problems, communicate again and again about the tools you're using to deal with them. In doing so you'll create a community of trust.
- **Embrace the pastoral leadership that's essential in deaning.** We don't talk enough about the quiet moments—the times we spend thinking about the difficulties facing individual students, individual faculty, alumni donors. But the pastoral role of the dean is among the most important aspects of the position. In times of complexity and times of difficulty, taking the time to listen to the people that we're supporting is essential. By embracing the pastoral role and balancing it with the role of the bully pulpit, we can make a real difference for the people we serve.
- **Be mindful of your team and your role on that team through teaching and research.** At the best, we are members of our own team, and it takes our leadership team within our college or department to succeed in bringing these changes. We are much more effective if we are part of the team than if we see ourselves (or our team members see us) as a step above their roles. So continue to teach, continue to do research, and participate as a peer as often as possible. That work builds a bridge back to your team, makes you more accessible, and helps you understand the truths that people may not want to share with a leader but are willing to share with a peer. Playing that role is important to maintaining cohesion within your group.
- **Be sure you're managing the flow of information.** There is a constant flow of misinformation in every higher education institution. One cannot stamp that out, but one can overwhelm it with accurate information that's being shared from a central source. The more you communicate effectively, the more you can counter misinformation.

- **Finally, support the core business of your university and college.** I always return to our dual missions of teaching and research, that at the beginning and end of any analysis we always return to the same questions: Is this what's best for our students? Is this what makes our students most successful? Is this what makes our work as scholars and researchers most impactful and makes the biggest difference in what we're doing? Those two fundamentals haven't changed in a thousand years, and they'll drive the success or failure of all the internal and external changes that we're looking at.

This article is adapted from the Magna 20-Minute Mentor *How Do I Lead Change from the Middle?*

Expectation for Continuous Improvement Even during Challenging Fiscal Times

N. Douglas Lees

Having a commitment to continuous improvement is an essential characteristic for effective department leadership (Lees et al. 2009). The process of making changes, both incremental and sweeping, that generate better outcomes, increased satisfaction, or enhanced efficiency is an expectation we have for our academic leaders. Promoting an agenda for improvement plays out differently based on a number of parameters, including whether the administrator is new or a veteran in the position, whether the individual was an internal or external hire, the current condition of the unit, and the resources available to the individual.

The new administrator

Having interviewed for the job and studied many aspects of the position, the new chair, dean, or provost will have some idea about what should be changed and will have articulated these ideas to those at the institution as part of the vetting process. Internal appointments might be able to discern weaknesses, but the remedies suggested by the internal individual might be more constrained by notions such as "We can't/don't do that here."

Although incoming administrators may have a long list of change items, they should address an achievable subset of these at the outset. Beginning too many projects at the same time makes tracking progress more difficult and taxes the available infrastructure. One consideration is that the new administrator will want to avoid a failed initiative; detractors will remember and remind others about it.

Some of the items on the change list should be easy ones that can give the individual early wins. For example, the new provost who has identified "enhancing research collaborations" as a target for improvement can create a new grants program that stimulates that activity. A new dean who has identified increasing online offerings as a goal could stimulate faculty by offering release time and small grants for course development. At the department level, a new chair could use the resource package to make graduate teaching assistant stipends more attractive and competitive, thereby improving the quality of the graduate student population and the instruction offered.

Having some timely solutions to recognized issues allows the administrator to demonstrate progress on the agenda for change. It also allows time to work on those thorny areas where improvement is needed. The examples of easy targets for change are those that require only the insight of how to make them happen and can be implemented unilaterally. In contrast, modifying promotion and tenure guidelines and changing the undergraduate curriculum are long-term items for improvement for deans and chairs, respectively.

Another example of a long-term goal that would be applicable to all levels of administration is the development of a strategic plan. Such a goal may involve impinging on the institutional mission, changing unit culture, and negotiating with multiple groups or "owners." Thus, change will take much more time and will likely result in challenging conversations, trade-offs, and assurances. The bottom line is that the agenda for change should be balanced with entries from the simple and quick to the complex, political, and long-term challenges.

The condition of the unit is an element the new administrator will also want to consider. A smoothly running institution, school, or department offering widely respected and innovative programs and with highly satisfied students, faculty, staff, and administration is at one end of the spectrum, whereas a failing unit with diminishing student numbers, an antiquated curriculum that is not well delivered, and unhappy constituents lies at the other.

The incoming administrator in the first case is challenged to find a way to make a positive difference, while in the latter the question is, "What do I do first?" The first case results in an evenly paced life with a low potential for substantial, positive change, while the second yields a frantic dash to get many elements running well and has a high delta for improvement.

The veteran administrator

Administrators no longer have start-up resources, and severe budget restrictions are often in place. In most institutions, dollars flow downhill; higher-level administrators have the first opportunity at resources, and department chairs have the last. For this reason, my focus is now on the department and chair levels.

A chair who is committed to continuous improvement will monitor all aspects of the department, seeking opportunities where changes can be made that will lead to better outcomes. This can mean course scheduling changes to increase student access, interventions to improve retention, policy tweaks to enhance research productivity, or changes to improve student recruitment, including developing a new degree track or program. Some of these changes will have a high price tag, resulting in them being set aside awaiting better times unless there is an external funding source to which a grant proposal could be submitted.

Some things, however, can be done to generate positive outcomes at minimal cost. It is during times when things look bleak and morale is low (e.g., lack of resources, no new or replacement hires) that making progress or improvements can make a real difference. This is also a time for the chair to demonstrate creativity and strong leadership by boldly moving ahead with priorities that make some aspect of department life better for faculty, staff, or students.

What types of improvements can be made inexpensively? Altering the scheduling of classes to increase access may not incur a monetary cost, although some faculty may object. This can both increase general student satisfaction and result in additional income from increased enrollments. Are you tired of those dreary old bulletin boards, or does your web site need updating? There is often hidden expertise among faculty and staff (or their families) unrelated to their professional work. If not, contact the art department and see if a student needs a project to meet degree requirements. Once identified, have the student work with staff to create a new look for the department's branding. The same approach with the website may be possible—this time working through the computer science or technology departments on campus.

Other examples include developing an online advising tool for majors or recruitment newsletters for high school students; hosting an undergraduate research poster day; and fostering meetings among department faculty and faculty from across campus and beyond to explore possible collaborations in teaching, engagement, and research. Some of these initiatives are substantial in their academic impact whereas others are cosmetic; however, all represent improvements, and all can lift the spirits of those who interact with students on a daily basis.

Creating an environment where there is continuous activity designed to make things better will eventually lead to faculty expecting to hear of the completion of one project (or at least a progress report) and the launch of another. The chair could entertain suggestions from faculty, staff, and students for improvement projects. The suggestions could then be vetted at a department meeting for cost, feasibility, and impact, and those scoring well could then be passed to the appropriate individuals for implementation.

The chair should regularly report to the department faculty and staff about the completion of improvement projects. Communication, especially about changes that affect students or the primary missions of the institution, should also be sent to upper administration. Administration will remember that the department accomplished much with relatively little and will perhaps be generous when future resources are available.

Reference
Lees, N. Douglas, David J. Malik, and Gautam Vemuri. 2009. "The Essentials of Chairing Academic Departments." *The Department Chair* 20(2): 1–3.

Can Innovation Be Taught?

Jeffrey L. Buller

As budgets tighten at colleges and universities, academic leaders are repeatedly urged to be more entrepreneurial in their approaches. "It's time to think outside the box," we're told. "Be creative. Be daring. Be innovative." But what do you do if you're not a naturally innovative person? Or how can you be creative if the people who work in your area rarely seem to display much creativity? In short, can innovation be taught? And even if it is taught, can it be *learned*?

In its most general sense, innovation is the ability to identify new or unexpected patterns and possibilities. For this reason, anyone—even the person whose thoughts seem to gravitate to the tried and true, outmoded, and familiar—can learn to become more innovative if the conditions are right. Our task as academic leaders is then to provide the right conditions. As the Dutch visionary Alexander den Heijer observed, "When a flower doesn't bloom, you fix the environment in which it grows, not the flower." In much the same way, fostering innovation isn't as much about teaching individuals as it is about creating a climate where new ideas are welcomed and explored.

Encourage many ideas

The first impediment to innovation is self-censorship. People tend to think that their ideas aren't worth sharing. It's similar to what we observe when children first start to draw or play a musical instrument: if their initial attempts are praised, no matter how rudimentary they may be, they tend to continue and eventually get better; if their initial attempts are mocked, they quickly assume that they're "just not good at this" and stop trying. As the two-time Nobel Prize-winning chemist Linus Pauling once observed, "If you want to have good ideas, you must have many ideas."

If you're working with individuals in a program that has not previously been known for its creativity, don't be too dismissive of their first efforts to think in new ways. If you criticize those attempts too harshly, you eliminate any likelihood that better ideas will come along later.

Relax the rules

The second impediment to innovation is perceived external censorship. People say things like, "We can't do that because the policy says we have to do it this way." As academic leaders, one of our primary roles should be not just to impose the rules when we have to but also to relax the rules whenever we can. Ask "What if?" and "Why not?" questions frequently. Eliminate red tape to whatever extent you can. Go over the policies in effect in your area and phase out any that no longer seem to be serving a useful purpose. Get permission for exceptions from your supervisor. Remember that an academic leader's chief responsibility is to be the chief exception maker, not the chief rule enforcer. If the job were simply to cite the policies, your job wouldn't be necessary. All the school would need is a policy manual and a list of sanctions for refusing to follow it. People are more innovative when they don't feel constrained by lots of rules and restrictions. Clear their path toward progress.

Encourage calculated risks

The third impediment to innovation is fear of failure. But innovation is fostered by academic leaders, not academic managers. Allow people to take a chance every now and then. But remember, in order for a calculated risk to be defensible when challenged by naysayers, it must first be *calculated*. Never take a risk on something you can't afford to lose. (It may be a good idea to risk your entire marketing budget on a new advertising strategy in the last quarter of the fiscal year, but not the first.) Never take too many risks simultaneously—if none of them pan out, you've got a disaster; if your results are successful, you may never really know which risk worked out the best. Always have a Plan B in case Plan A ends in failure. And always have a rationale in case you're challenged about the wisdom of your strategy.

Be experimental

The fourth impediment to innovation is uncertainty. If we knew for sure that an idea was going to yield good results, we wouldn't hesitate to implement it. But the uncertainty of whether we might look brilliant or foolish for embarking on a plan can paralyze some people. So even though it's unwise to take more than one risk simultaneously, it can often be beneficial to conduct more than one experiment simultaneously. As the saying goes, "Dip your toe in the water before plunging right in." We do something similar in higher education all the time. We run a course (or even several variations of a course) under a Special Topics designation before permanently changing the curriculum. We hire someone (or even several people) on a temporary basis before we issue an ongoing contract. So if you're uncertain about an idea, offer it "adjunct" or "visiting" status before you "tenure" it. Try a short trial run, tweak the idea on the basis of your results, and then decide whether to implement the idea in a more expanded manner, revise it yet again, or abandon it entirely.

Depressurize the environment

Some people work well under tight deadlines and when there's a great deal at stake. But most people don't. They become unwilling to try something new or even to feel free enough to *think* of something new when they're operating under great stress. So do whatever you can to eliminate unnecessary pressure. Distinguish carefully between when sanctions for missing a deadline or failing to reach a goal are truly necessary and when the results are merely annoying, even though no great harm is done. Look at your work environment and try to determine where harsh lighting, cluttered desks, stark white or industrial gray walls, metal furniture, unattractive wall décor, and other elements are conveying an image of "this is a place of efficiency and toil" instead of "this is a place of creativity and innovation." Consider how the tone of your own voice or the style of your own email messages may be producing the sort of stress that stifles experimentation and freedom of thought. Redefine your role as someone who helps others achieve their goals (even their *dreams*) instead of as someone who just gets the job done on time and under budget.

Be patient

In short, it's unlikely that a previously uncreative person will suddenly become innovative because of something that you teach or a technique that you develop. But by rethinking what it means to be an academic leader, you can create an environment that, over time, begins generating first ideas, then good ideas, and finally great ideas. If we want others to become more creative and innovative, we must first lead creatively and innovatively.

Leading Your Academic Department toward Inclusion: How to Ensure Faculty Are LGBTQ+ Competent in the Classroom

Timothy R. Bussey

During my six years at the University of Connecticut, I had the opportunity to interact with many different faculty members across our campus community. This was particularly true during my final two years, when I coordinated our Rainbow Center's Out to Lunch (OTL) Lecture Series. The OTL Lecture Series—our center's largest and most attended recurring program—hosted fellow academics and community advocates, whose work dealt with contemporary intersectional issues and topics related to the LGBTQ+ community. While the OTL Lecture Series had served as a key fixture to the Rainbow Center's programming for many years, we soon identified that it had missed opportunities in one key demographic on our campus: faculty.

Throughout the next two years, we worked to ensure that the OTL Lecture Series would become a program that also appealed to faculty, while the Rainbow Center also engaged more outreach to this segment of our campus community. Considering our work and the recent changes in federal educational policies pertaining to transgender students, using the OTL Lecture Series as a way to engage faculty around LGBTQ+ cultural competency soon became another key priority for managing the program. I'm happy to share that, throughout my two years with the Rainbow Center, we had numerous positive interactions with faculty, who had previously never come to our center or actively engaged queer topics in their classroom or research. These positive experiences and my perspective on how they were attained are the basis for this article about how to ensure faculty are LGBTQ+ competent in the classroom.

1. Assess what your faculty know *and* need, regarding LGBTQ+ competency in the classroom. While you certainly want to be attuned to national and regional issues affecting queer and transgender students, a best practice is assessing what your faculty already know about the LGBTQ+ community before deciding what they need. In assessing this level of knowledge, I'd also recommend being aware of certain things like social desirability bias—a type of response bias where the respondent provides an answer that they hope will be viewed more favorably. In short, you want to ensure that you obtain a clear picture of what your faculty members know and being cognizant of potential issues of response bias can be helpful in getting truly accurate information about their existing knowledge and needs. For instance, you could use an anonymous forum to gauge how much your faculty know about LGBTQ+ issues, which can then assist you in developing and/or identifying trainings and resources that are useful to the faculty within your department.

2. Identify training and educational opportunities that are internal and external to your campus community. Once you have assessed your faculty's knowledge and needs, you can then use that information to identify various training and educational opportunities both within and around your campus community. For campuses with offices or centers specializing in supporting diverse student demographics, many of these spaces have safe zone or safe space trainings, which introduce basic concepts relevant to supporting and empathizing with LGBTQ+ students. In addition to this, there are, of course, a number of other external opportunities. To aid you in considering the available possibilities for advancing your faculty's level of LGBTQ+ cultural competency, I've listed a variety of such opportunities here: online, queer-specific Title IX trainings from the Association of Title IX Administrators; regional and national LGBTQ+ education and inclusivity conferences like the Creating Change Conference; specialized, discipline-specific trainings that can be offered by colleagues at other institutions; and listservs like the one offered through the Consortium of Higher Education LGBT Resource Professionals.

3. Motivate faculty to engage with queer and trans specific issues and topics in multiple settings. Once you have identified various training and educational opportunities for your faculty, a best practice is to motivate them to engage such resources when possible. While it may be tempting to encourage a number of simultaneous opportunities, this can be overwhelming for some faculty, and depending on your departmental culture, it may prove more effective to stagger the presentation of such opportunities throughout the academic year. In fact, staggering these trainings throughout the year can help your faculty stay more mindful of their queer and transgender students, which will further ensure that your department is moving in a more inclusive direction. As a rule, you'll also want to ensure that you convey the complex and nuanced issues that can face LGBTQ+ students in a college classroom, such as ensuring correct pronoun usage, providing consistent representation in the curriculum, maintaining a healthy and open classroom environment, etc. This can further emphasize that true classroom inclusivity for LGBTQ+ students isn't derived from one simple solution, training, or best practice.

4. Recognize that increased cultural competency should build over time and work to keep your faculty members informed about current trends. As mentioned, there are several issues that can face queer and transgender students, and these can vary across intersectional identities within the community. Your faculty also might encounter LGBTQ+ students who face challenges both inside and outside of the classroom at any point during their academic careers, and your department will likely never be able to host a training to prepare faculty for every challenge that they might encounter. As such, I'd recommend that you be transparent with faculty members and explain that you hope to envision a departmental culture that will build this increased cultural competency consistently over time. This can assist faculty with anticipating your expectations, while also affirming your commitment to leading your department into a more LGBTQ+ inclusive direction. This final point will also help faculty remain cognizant that many issues facing queer and transgender college students—like the application of Title IX to transgender students—can change rapidly and without much prior notice. Given this reality, it is best to recognize that the work of inclusion is a continual process, rather than something that can be achieved in a single training session. With that in mind, there should be a continued expectation that faculty consider the multiple ways that they can support their LGBTQ+ students in any given course.

Laying the Groundwork for Positive, Voluntary Technology Changes

Stephanie Delaney

When it comes to voluntary technological change—that is, change that you want to do to move your college forward or help people integrate useful new pedagogies—people respond differently. One message isn't going to work for all people. You've got to tailor the message to different constituencies.

When I talk about being a leader of technological change, I mean the person who sets the stage for the change, who creates the direction for the change, who has the big idea and brings that to everybody at the campus, and who gets them to get on board with that big idea and want to follow along.

Now, that doesn't mean that the person needs to be an administrator or a supervisor or the leader of their team. Anybody on campus can lead the technological change. Again, the change I'm talking about is voluntary change, which is often innovative change. It's change where you're setting the stage, where you're doing something different than what's been done before or applying something, maybe, that's been successful someplace else—something that's been done before, but putting it in a new setting or trying to achieve a different goal with it.

And innovative change takes a kind of vision that not everybody shares. Not everybody is able to see a path to a place where you don't know where you're going. So when you're trying to be a leader of that kind of change, you want to be able to paint a picture of where that some place might be, especially if you don't have other colleges to say, "Oh, look, this college did it and they were successful," or "This college did it and they had these outcomes." No, you're that college. You are the people who are going to say,

"This is what we want it to be. We can paint the picture of being whatever we want." And I think that that ability to paint that picture is the important role of the leader in introducing technological change.

What campus technology leaders can do

When you think about a technology leader on campus, there are a few things you look to that person to do. One thing is to disseminate useful information. It could be that you're reading things that other people aren't reading and then sharing those articles with people when you see that it might be useful to something that they're doing. It could be that you are getting studies about information that's really useful to people. So you're bringing in things that other people may not be seeing and you're sharing it out with them in a way that's accessible and useful. So that's one thing we look to technological leaders to do: inform us about what we need to know about technology.

The other thing that we look to technological leaders to do is to help other leaders on campus make technology choices. For example, if your school is considering adopting a new learningmanagement system, and you have choice A, B, and C, how do they choose? What sorts of things do they need to consider? Who do they need to have at the table? How do they need to make that decision? A good technological leader on campus can help other leaders make those decisions and make them wisely in a way that will be well-accepted by other people on the campus.

Another thing that a good technological leader can do is cultivate a change-friendly environment. And that means not just saying no when you don't know how things are going to turn out. It's also helping to create a buffer between the people with the innovative ideas and the people who just say no, and helping to create a bridge between those two groups. Because really, the people who just say no are not mean people, they're not people without vision. They are people who want to make sure that everything goes right.

And if you ask them, "Hey, let's try this new thing," and they can't immediately envision how it's all going to go right, the response will be no. But that response is often an invitation for additional conversation. It may be that if you keep working with the no person, eventually they're able to work through it, and you get to yes. Again, it's that patience, that working together with someone. And so being a person who understands how to get no to yes and how to create a buffer between the innovators and the naysayers—that's a really important role of a change leader, and a really important part of cultivating a change-friendly environment.

Case study: MOOC mania at Seattle Central College

I want to share a story with you about a voluntary technological change that you might be able to use as an example while you're sort of thinking through how this might work on your own campus. Several years ago, you'll remember, MOOCs were all the rage. Just as they were becoming all the rage, Canvas, which is the learning management system we use at Seattle Central College, introduced a MOOC platform called the Canvas Network. And they invited a bunch of colleges to participate in having the very first classes on the MOOC Campus Network.

And so we decided to do that. And we put up a US history class that was in a MOOC format. And this was very new. Nobody else in our state was offering a MOOC. We were the only community college that was on the Canvas Network. And we were really excited to be trying this new and exciting thing.

MOOC mania was everywhere. Platforms were coming out. You had Udacity, you had all these different things, and so we wanted to get in at the beginning of that. And we didn't have anything that said some sort of success will come of a community college putting up a class and making it into a MOOC, but we wanted to try it. We wanted to see what would happen.

Our first US history course had a bunch of people take it. Over 1,000 students signed up from all over the world! I was really surprised. I didn't expect it to have such penetration, that so many people were eager to learn about US history, a subject that many people think is a little bit dry, a little bit boring. But these people were coming in and were taking the class, and round after round. The class would run for about six weeks, and then it would start again because there was just such demand for it. It was really very amazing. After a couple of years, however, interest started to peter out. And before long, we decided to cancel the class. So was that MOOC a success or not? The answer depends on what our goals were when we started the class.

We had a few specific goals for trying this class. One was just advertising for Seattle Central. Not everybody had heard of our college or our district, and this was a great way to get our name out there. Another one was to try something new. Like I mentioned, this was the beginning of the MOOC mania, and here was an opportunity for us to try, without too much risk, something new.

We also wanted to serve our local community. I mean, we are a community college serving all of the people in our area. And with the MOOC, we were able to serve people not only in our immediate geographic area but also throughout the state of Washington, and indeed, throughout the entire nation, helping people to learn more about US history. And as we saw once we put the course up, helping people all over the world to learn more about US history. And that just was really powerful.

So those were our goals. We might ask also what were the goals of the student? When you hear about MOOCs, often the first thing that people say to you about them is, "Oh, well, this huge number of students never actually finished the course." Well, guess what? That was not the goal of the students. They weren't taking this course to finish the course. They were taking this course to sort of dip their toes into US history. They just wanted to learn a little bit, and most of them achieved what it was they wanted to learn. And I think that's exciting.

So we did have some specific goals that we wanted to achieve, and we did achieve them. We shared out with lots of people who had never heard about Seattle Central College. They knew about Seattle Central. Our community was served, not only our local community, but as you saw, the global community was served by sharing this course. We were able to try something new, and see that there were different ways to offer the traditional correspondence course in a way that reached people in a really more engaging way than we had done it before. So all of those things we achieved.

We don't know really whether we achieved the enrollment goal. We didn't have a way of tracking that well, so we never found out whether enrollments increased. My guess is no. That maybe one or two new students came to the college, if that. But the other goals that we had were met, and that's exciting. And I think what's even more exciting, though, is that the students who were taking the course, their goals were met. A few students did finish through to the end. We were able to track that because we gave students the opportunity to request certificates of completion. And so we were able to track how many students were asking for those.

But it was great to see both students and the college achieve what they wanted. So here's an example of a voluntary technological change, experimenting with something new, innovating in a way that didn't have any sort of example. We couldn't point to another community college and say, "They did a MOOC, and they achieved these outcomes, so we can do it too." No, we were the example. People pointed to us and said, "Hey, Seattle Central did it. Let's do it too." And that's what ended up happening. Several other community colleges decided to do MOOCs on a variety of subjects, and you know had a measure of success all because they were able to point to us and say, "Look, they could do it, so we could do it too."

Steps for introducing voluntary technology change

When I first started thinking about how to strategically introduce voluntary technological change, I decided to look at different frameworks for change, different strategies about change. And there are lots of them out there. There are so many books on introducing change to an organization. Yet none of them really fit what I was trying to do. So I decided to throw them all out and just create my own framework, outlined below.

The first step is to think about what change you want to introduce. Make sure it's an elective change—something that you're doing because you want to do it. Additionally, make sure that the change will suit your organization, that you've thoughtfully considered the change you're going to introduce.

Next, you'll want to bring a bunch of voices to the table and brainstorm. This step is crucial because one of the biggest complaints people have about changes that are introduced is that nobody asked them. *Why didn't they look at how this was going to impact my area? Why didn't anybody consider my concerns?* This first step of brainstorming allows you to bring a lot of people to the table in informal ways.

And it doesn't need to be everyone at one table all at once. In fact, I'd recommend a series of small conversations where you're going to different areas of the college that might be affected and talking to them about the changes that you want to introduce, how they feel about those changes, their concerns, and how they think the changes could be helpful. And really listen to those concerns. Eeyores—those who say, "Oh, it'll never work," "This is going to be a disaster," "It's going to cost so much"—are your friends. Listen to those people because while they're not always right, they always have a point that you should pay attention to. Listen to those people and figure out an answer to every single one of their concerns before you move forward. Other people are going to raise those issues too, so those Eeyores' concerns are your pathway to a successful strategy. So when you do the brainstorming, make sure you really listen to all of the voices, and when you're done, ask people who else you should contact and then talk to them.

This brainstorming step could take a long time depending on the size of your organization, but it is time well spent. If you skip it, you will fail. Your change is not going to work if you don't incorporate as many voices as possible. And you don't have to do all the things that people suggest, but you need to at least acknowledge for them that they have been heard and their concerns will be addressed. That's key to successful implementation.

After you've done the brainstorming and gotten everyone's input, the next step is to set achievable goals. Why is it that you're doing it and why?

Make sure your goals are achievable and measurable. You saw in my example that we didn't have a way to track whether our enrollment increased. We could only measure how many students finished the MOOC, at least through their requests for certificates of completion. And so it's important that you have achievable goals and can determine whether you've attained them.

The final step is to celebrate success. When (not if) everything works out and you're a huge success, have a party. Send celebratory emails. Recognize people. Give them flowers. Do something to celebrate the fact that it was a success. This serves a couple of purposes. It lets people know that (1) this instance of risk-taking had a beneficial end and (2) people who take risks can indeed be rewarded. So often risk takers are not rewarded; in fact, they're harmed in some way, especially if they fail. But you want to celebrate the success and make sure that lots of people know that what you guys tried worked out.

What happens if the change is not successful? What if what you tried doesn't work out the way you wanted it to? The first thing you want to do is acknowledge that. Don't ignore it; don't bury it under the carpet. Don't just pretend that the innovative activity never happened, because that's going to discourage people when you want to try something new again. They're not going to want to try it, because the last time didn't turn out so well.

You'll want to be open about that lack of success and say what you learned from it. Maybe that's another round of brainstorming. "Hey, we tried this, what did we learn? What can we pull out of this?" And then celebrate what you learned as its own kind of success. Because really, if you're not failing on a fairly regular basis, then you're not trying as hard as you could. You're not being very innovative if you are always succeeding. So you need to create a culture of learning from failure and celebrating risk-taking. That way, when you go on to the next innovative change that you want to introduce to your campus, people are going to be more willing to go out on a limb and try something new.

This article is adapted from the Magna 20-Minute Mentor, *How Can I Lay the Groundwork for Positive Technology Changes?*

From Fringe to Mainstream: Increasing the Acceptance of Online Education on Your Campus

Brian Udermann

Overall, colleges and universities continue to expand the number of online courses and degree programs they offer. But even with the continued growth in online programming, significant resistance to online education persists on many campuses. This resistance can come from faculty, staff, students, and administrators. This article explores five strategies to increase the acceptance of online education on campus.

1. Get faculty involved

One strategy that can help increase the acceptance of online education on campus is to involve faculty early and often in online education initiatives. This involvement can take many forms. One idea is to create an online advisory group or online education committee and make sure there is strong faculty representation in that group. When I became the director of online education on my campus 12 years ago, one of the first things I did was create an online advisory group. Proposed initiatives or policies and procedures related to online education would originate from that group, not from me. The campus community was more receptive to supporting and moving forward with online education initiatives because of the faculty involvement in those decisions. Another idea to get faculty involved is to have them take the lead on matters like new online program development. Proposing a new online program, especially if it is the first one offered on campus, can be a tricky and even contentious process. Having a faculty member (rather than, say, an administrator) lead that effort can make for a smoother approval process. Some institutions provide a small incentive for this work, such as a stipend or course release.

2. Be responsive to faculty concerns

I've yet to interact with an online education administrator who has said that when their institution decided to explore more online programming or move forward with a large online initiative, the faculty were 100 percent onboard. Faculty will have concerns. Those concerns often relate to the rigor or quality of online education, academic integrity, workload and compensation, intellectual property, a reduction in student credit hour production in face-to-face courses or programs, new policies and procedures specific to online education, online education taking over the campus, and the eventual closure of the brick-and-mortar institution. Many online administrators are tuned in and aware of what concerns the faculty on their campuses; however, it doesn't hurt to ask. Consider surveying faculty to determine what their major concerns about or barriers to online education might be. Host campus open forums where faculty can express their views. Attend faculty governance committee meetings when discussions about online education are on the agenda. Additionally, have as many conversations as possible with individual faculty and solicit their views about online learning. Years ago, when my institution was first attempting to grow our online courses and programs, I would block off one hour per week to walk around campus with the aim of talking to as many faculty as I could.

3. Focus on quality, not growth

Over the years I've seen many higher ed administrators panic because they felt like they were falling behind their peers or competition in regard to the number of online courses and programs they offered. Sometimes this panicked state results in unwise decisions to quickly forge ahead with large online initiatives even though faculty may be unprepared to teach online, student support services offices may be unable to adequately support online learners, and the overall institutional infrastructure to support online education may not exist. I've also seen administrators start crunching numbers and making growth and revenue production their primary motivation to expand online programing. Faculty are usually more receptive to the expansion of online education if they believe the motivation for doing so is to better serve students while making quality the focal point. Much could be written about ensuring quality in online programming, but let me share one strategy that has greatly helped my institution: hire exceptional faculty support personnel, such as instructional designers, instructional technologists, eLearning specialists, and media specialists. These are the folks who often work the closest with faculty, helping them with issues such as mastering the learning management system, online course design and facilitation, and best practices in online teaching.

4. Offer high-quality professional development opportunities for faculty

Fear often comes with the unknown, and some faculty fear making the transition to teaching online because they know little to nothing about online instruction. Not feeling prepared to teach online can be a major hurdle or barrier to faculty deciding to design and develop an online course. That's where offering high-quality professional development opportunities can help. These opportunities can range from one-to-one consultations between instructional designers and faculty to workshops or seminars offered through an institution's teaching and learning center to multi-weeklong online instructor training courses or certifications. While qualified faculty support personnel often lead these sessions, it's been my experience that having experienced online instructors help with or lead professional development opportunities for those interested in online teaching is particularly effective. As I like to say, "Who better to influence a tenured professor who has been teaching on your campus for 30 years and is resistant to online education than a tenured professor who has been teaching on your campus for 30 years and is having great success with teaching online?" Also, institutions will need to decide whether to develop these opportunities in-house, use an outside company or vendor, or do both. And some institutions provide faculty incentives for completing professional development opportunities, especially longer trainings or certifications.

5. Provide strong student support services for online learners

Giving online students the help and support they need to succeed in class comes with benefits such as increased student satisfaction, improved retention, and heightened academic achievement. Greater student support usually precedes greater student success. It's important to attempt to determine and plan for the types of help and services online learners will need. This shouldn't be an afterthought to launching a large online education initiative; it should be discussed at the outset. Units and offices that can influence student success include admissions, records and registration, financial aid, academic advising, career services, counseling and testing, the tutoring center, information technology services, the library, student life, the multicultural support center, and many more. Online learners should receive exceptional support from the time they contact admissions to inquire about the institution to the time they graduate. Online learners should be afforded the same services as on-campus students; this has become a regional accreditation expectation. I recommend that someone on campus—often it is the primary online administrator—periodically reach out to the directors of units and offices that support students and review the services they provide to online learners.

Five Strategies to Improve the Quality of Online Education on Your Campus

Brian Udermann

It can be difficult to discuss the quality of online education as what constitutes quality is a complex issue and no single agreed-upon definition exists. Many factors can come into play when discussing the quality of online offerings, such as course design and facilitation, student academic achievement, student and faculty satisfaction, and retention. I've served as the director of online education at the University of Wisconsin–La Crosse since 2007, and I believe the five strategies outlined in this article have helped us elevate the quality of our online courses and programs.

1. Provide exceptional professional development opportunities for faculty

Faculty often say that a major barrier to developing and teaching online courses is that they don't feel prepared to do so. One way to counter that concern is to provide high-quality professional development opportunities related to online learning. This can be done in a variety of ways—for instance, by offering one-on-one consultations with faculty, workshops through an institution's teaching center, or an online instructor training course. Some institutions also have mentoring programs in which experienced online instructors mentor those just getting started teaching online. Another strategy we often recommend to faculty who are exploring the idea of teaching online is to see whether a colleague who is a veteran online instructor would be willing to add them to an existing online course. This gives the inexperienced faculty member a chance to see, for example, how an online course is set up and how an experienced online instructor successfully facilitates a course, and it can alleviate some of the fears or concerns new online instructors might have. Institutions will also want to discuss whether they will create these professional development opportunities in-house, use outside vendors, or do both.

2. Hire appropriate faculty support personnel

Over the past five to 10 years, colleges and universities have been expanding the number of online courses and degree programs they offer. Part of what has made this expansion possible is the hiring of individuals to guide and train faculty on the best practices of online course development and facilitation. The titles of these support personnel are varied and can include instructional designer, instructional technologist, media specialist, e-learning coach, e-learning developer, and learning strategist, among others. I've chaired five search and screen committees over the past 10 years to hire five instructional designers at my institution and will offer the following recommendation: Be clear on why the institution it is hiring a faculty support professional and what that person will be doing. Will their primary role consist of staying in their office for much of the day and building online course content? So, more of a production specialist. Will their role be to train faculty through one-on-one interactions, workshops, and training courses? In that case, they will likely have much more interaction with faculty. It's also important during the hiring process that the support professional is clear on what will be expected of them should they accept a position at the institution.

3. Implement a quality course review process

Another strategy to help ensure the quality of online courses is to utilize a course review process prior to online classes being taught. A variety of course review rubrics exist; some, such as Quality Matters, are fee based, while others are openly available. It is also becoming increasingly common for institutions to create their own course review standards or guidelines. It is important to determine who will do the reviews. Sometimes reviews are done by faculty peers, sometimes by department chairs, and other times by faculty support personnel such as instructional designers. Often the results or feedback from a course review are shared with faculty in writing, but I suggest scheduling a face-to-face meeting with faculty to discuss the results of a review. We do approximately 40 online course reviews per year at my institution; for each review, two instructional designers and I meet with the faculty member and go through our course evaluation guidelines, share what we thought the instructor did well in regard to course development, and usually offer the instructor a half dozen or so suggestions or recommendations for revisions or improvements.

4. Consider a program- or institution-wide online education quality review

Reviewing online courses for quality prior to their being offered has occurred since the mid-1990s and become somewhat commonplace in higher education. While program- and institution-wide quality reviews are relatively new, they are starting to increase in frequency. A program- or institution-wide quality review is much more comprehensive in nature and often examines overarching areas such as institutional and administrative support for online learning, technology infrastructure, course design and development, learner support services, faculty support and development, and evaluation and assessment. These reviews can help university personnel identify strengths and weaknesses specific to online learning, which can be helpful in identifying new initiatives or priorities to consider. These reviews can also prove beneficial when determining resource allocation, creating an online education strategic plan, or preparing for a regional accreditation visit. Here are some options for a program- or institution-wide quality review:

- Online Learning Consortium Quality Scorecard for the Administration of Online Programs: https://onlinelearningconsortium.org/consult/olc-quality-scorecard-suite
- Quality Matters Program Certification Overview: https://www.qualitymatters.org/qm-reviews-certifications/program-reviews
- United States Distance Learning Association Distance Learning Quality Standards Certification: https://usdla.org/certification
- University Professional and Continuing Education Association Hallmarks of Excellence in Online Leadership: https://upcea.edu/resources/hallmarks-online

5. Keep the focus on quality, not revenue generation

Over the past 12 years, I've interacted with many university administrators who felt like they were falling behind other institutions in the number of online courses and programs they offered. Frequently, the conversation would turn to revenue generation and how much money these institutions were "missing out on" because of a lack of online programming. These administrators, sometimes in a panicked state, often forged ahead with large online education initiatives without having the necessary pedagogical, technological, or administrative infrastructure in place to support online learning. Having worked in higher education for the past 20 years as both a faculty member and an administrator, I've observed that faculty are a pretty perceptive bunch. They can usually deduce when the motivation for expanding online learning is simply to generate more revenue, and that is not always well received. Taking the necessary steps to ensure the quality of online programming, a number of which are outlined in this article, will go a long way in helping with faculty buy-in and improving the culture of acceptance related to online learning on campus.

Accessibility: Making a Plan to Do What's Right (and Required)

Vance S. Martin

As of 2017, the last full year we have data for, there were 5,567 Office of Civil Rights (OCR) investigations dealing with accessibility in K–20 institutions (Department of Education, 2019, p. Z-22). In 2018, Americans with Disabilities Act (ADA) Title III Lawsuits in federal courts were projected to hit almost 10,000 (Vu, Launey, Ryan, & Fitz, 2018). These numbers have been increasing each year—almost exponentially for ADA lawsuits. I've been working with digital accessibility issues since 2007. Until recently, much of what I've warned about in meetings and conversations was ignored, making me feel like Cassandra from Greek myth. But in the past few years, teachers and administrators have begun to ask what we need to do, and some institutions are preparing to act. The University of Illinois Springfield (UIS) is one of those institutions, so I am offering our lessons to help others move forward.

Why do we need to make content accessible? A simple answer is that making our teaching materials, marketing materials, and our forms usable by anyone who comes across them online is the right thing to do. Of course, doing what's right can get overtaken by everything else vying for our time, including advising, meetings, grading, and family. At which point the law steps in to remind us that yes, what's right is also compulsory. So what are the laws?

Four main federal laws govern accessibility within education. The first is the Rehabilitation Act of 1973, specifically section 504, which prohibits programs that receive federal funds from discriminating against people with disabilities. In 1986, Section 508 was added with guidelines for making information technology accessible; however, these guidelines only became binding in 1998. In 1990, the ADA was signed; it extended the guidelines of accessibility guaranteed under the 1973 law to private industry. In 1999, technology experts around the world devised their own accessibility guidelines, which became known as the Web Content Accessibility Guidelines (WCAG). These were revised in 2008 as WCAG 2.0. In 2010, the 21st Century Communications and Video Accessibility Act was passed and applied to making commercial videos accessible for those with hearing disabilities. Finally, Section 508 was refreshed in 2017 to account for all the changes to digital technology since 1998. On the whole, Section 508 points to WCAG as the guidelines to meet.

At this point, from a software standpoint, the what is easy: most major software packages used in higher education have built-in accessibility features that meet WCAG standards. Microsoft Word and PowerPoint have a built-in, easy-to-use accessibility checker that highlights and helps users fix most accessibility issues—provided that they actually use it (see here: https://support.microsoft.com/en-us/office/improve-accessibility-with-the-accessibility-checker-a16f6de0-2f39-4a2b-8bd8-5ad-801426c7f?). Adobe Acrobat also has built-in wizards and checkers, though these are less user-friendly and take more time to learn than Microsoft's (see here: https://www.adobe.com/accessibility/products/acrobat/using-acrobat-pro-accessibility-checker.html). Unless someone has access to the newest version and enough licenses for the entire community, these becomes problematic to use. Concerning video, YouTube is a cheap and easy way to caption videos and produce transcripts (see here: https://support.google.com/youtube/answer/2734796). Auto checkers are wonderful, but they will always require a final check by a human. Of course, the laws also cover websites and procurement of software and technology. This could relate to classroom response systems, publisher software that mimics a learning management system (LMS), or the newest app used in the classroom.

At UIS this work began more than five years ago, when the executive director of the Center for Online Learning, Research and Service and the associate vice chancellor for online learning leveraged the IT department to begin making our website accessible. This was a multiyear project and remains a struggle as the site's many users continue to upload inaccessible content, such as PDFs inaccessible to screen readers, or forget to add alternative text to images. The executive director and vice chancellor also began the process of hiring a campus accessibility specialist, which took some time. I came to UIS in this capacity in late 2017. Since then I have met with deans, department chairs, and faculty to discuss accessibility and train them on how to make materials accessible.

One concern faculty had was having the time amid all their other commitments to make files accessible. So, in early 2018 our executive director managed to secure funding for student workers to remediate faculty files. I was able to hire and train four student workers for this task. These students mostly work on Word docs, PowerPoints, PDFs, and videos. They were able to complete 919 files for 42 classes in their first semester and 890 files for 50 classes in their second. This totaled 4,471.25 minutes of videos, 7,544 PowerPoint slides, 10,177 PDF pages, and 2,701 Word pages. We paid four students about $11,000 for those two semesters of work. Each student worked about 20 hours per week each semester. Had we contracted with a commercial entity, based on local pricing, that would have been about $66,000. The work of student workers reduced this cost by 82 percent.

Over the past year or so, I've conducted many workshops and given many presentations on how to make materials accessible. In these workshops and presentations, I mention the success of my student workers, and I am often asked whether this approach could work at another school. The short answer is yes.

For institutions that have moved beyond why and what and onto how, here are my suggestions:

1. **Develop a school-wide policy.** Ours was officially adopted in March 2018 (see here: https://www.uis.edu/academicstaffhandbook/university-policies/digital-resource-accessibility-policy). Federal laws remain in place; you may even have a state law requiring accessibility as well. But if you were under an Office of Civil Rights investigation, they would first ask for and then look at your policy, which is another reason to have a policy.

2. **Decide who will oversee accessibility.** This team or committee should certainly include an administrator who has authority to act as well as someone in IT, a library representative, faculty, and staff. When selecting faculty or staff, look for those with some technology knowledge and those with institutional cultural capital. Even better is someone with both.

3. **Conduct an audit of all things digital, and come up with a plan or a timeline or both.** For an audit, figure out where all your digital files are. Files in your LMS, videos in your streaming service, web pages, publicly facing documents, and faculty files on the computers they use for class are a sampling. Some institutions may plan to start with the area with the least files and others with the same type of file; others still may focus on a specific area—web pages or the LMS, for example. An overall plan will include these as stages and say who is

responsible for doing the work. A timeline will take all the planned activities, determine how long each stage will take, and specify a date by which the area, files, or work will be done.
4. **Train, train, and train.** This will not be a one-time training. Some people may want to hear about the laws first, and some may want only to learn how to do something. Because only so much can be learned from each training session, people may attend the same workshop several times. Some people will be resistant, and new people will join the organization, so training will take a long time.
5. **Create support to help with materials.** It takes less than a semester to train a student worker to make materials accessible. Use student workers; they will learn great skills and can focus on the task without distraction. If you support the faculty and train them on how to make new content accessible, they will be thrilled that you're helping them play catch-up.
6. **Accept that accessibility will take time and money and lead to a culture change.** UIS covers my salary, student compensation, and minor costs for computers and a few specialized software licenses. There are about 4,500 colleges and universities and 16,000 school districts in the US. With a little over 5,000 OCR investigations each year, there is a one in four chance of your school being investigated. The costs of overtime and complying with the laws on a forced timeline far exceed the costs of systematically complying with the laws on your own timeline.
7. **Continue to think about areas of need.** Although we are currently continuing training and working on faculty files, we will tackle website PDFs this year. We will also look at faculty use of inaccessible publisher software. Last year we worked with the library, and they now make all course reserves, which are scanned PDFs, accessible. For schools with limited licenses of Adobe Acrobat, decreasing overall use of PDFs and centralizing PDF remediation in one place is a good idea. I have worked with schools that centralized this work in the library, the president's office, or the office in charge of online learning.

I predict that within a few years our student workers will work primarily on PDFs and videos. Most files we have received were Word and PowerPoint, which faculty and staff creators can easily fix. Videos and PDFs are a bit more time-consuming. I would also venture that within the next few years there will be more accessible software programs and more software with accessibility features built in. When I began in this area in 2007, there was no automated way to check Microsoft or Adobe files, and all facets of captioning were done by hand. At present I am not aware of a video player for a learning management system that meets all accessibility requirements, including audio descriptions.

Using students to remediate files at UIS has been very successful. I've heard only a few concerns, which come down to two questions. The first: *Can students, who aren't experts in a field work on the content in my field?* Yes, most remediation is structural, not content based. With several thousand files worked on, we've had to ask for faculty assistance on fewer than 30 files. The second: *What if I take the time to train a student and they leave the next semester?* I usually hear this from two-year institutions. In our first semester I was able to train four students to remediate the four main file types; by the end of the semester they needed only minimal oversight. Two of those students left the next semester, and I trained two more. With three to four busy weeks for me of training, a student working 20 hours per week can remediate the four main file types for the rest of a semester. Certainly their work improves each term, and the more semesters they stay, the less time I spend on training. If students stay for a few semesters, they can help train other student workers.

References

Department of Education. (2019). *Office of Civil Rights fiscal year 2020 budget request*. Retrieved from https://www2.ed.gov/about/overview/budget/budget20/justifications/z-ocr.pdf

Vu, M. N., Launey, K. M., Ryan S., & Fitz, K. (2018, July 17). Website access and other ADA Title III lawsuits hit record numbers. Retrieved from https://www.adatitleiii.com/2018/07/website-access-and-other-ada-title-iii-lawsuits-hit-record-numbers

How to Encourage Faculty to Adopt OER

John Orlando

The growth of open educational resources (OER) may prove transformative in the way online learning has been. Textbook costs have skyrocketed to the point that finding an alternative is no longer simply an issue of saving students money but of preserving educational outcomes as students forgo textbooks they cannot afford. A Virginia State University study found that, due to cost, only 47 percent of students purchase textbooks for their courses (Feldstein et. al., 2012).

Despite that low figure, Julia and Jeff Seaman found that only 9 percent of faculty use open resources in their courses (Seaman & Seaman, 2017). The problem is awareness. The faculty who use OER usually only do so because of a chance encounter with them at a conference or a colleague's recommendation. Institutions that want widespread adoption of open resources among faculty should formally implement programs to encourage faculty to add OER to their courses and support faculty efforts to do so. Luckily, a few schools have launched such programs, and these can serve as guides to other institutions looking to launch OER initiatives.

Finding open resources

Probably the biggest barriers to faculty adoption of open resources are lack of knowledge of where to find them and the perceived time required to search for them. Moreover, faculty commonly assume that OER will be of lesser quality than traditional textbooks—that the resources are compiled by novices rather than qualified academics and not vetted, which is not the case.

Thus, the first job of any institution looking to get faculty buy-in for open resources is education, and I suggest the library be given it rather than the IT department. Why? This is not a technical issue; it's a content and pedagogical issue. The library can put together a workshop for departments to demonstrate where and how to find open resources. Such a workshop could profile the many educational institutions offering OER, including MIT's Open Courseware program, the Open University, OpenStax at Rice University, and the Commonwealth of Learning OAsis. It might also address how many states and Canadian provinces are putting out open resources developed by colleges and universities and highlight the many repositories that aggregate OER from a variety of sources.

Far from a lack of resources, the reality is that there are so many OER that they can be overwhelming to search. For this reason, it is important to support faculty in searching open resources. The College of the Canyons solved this problem by hiring students and former students to search on faculty members' behalves (Lieberman, 2018). Today's students are well versed in search and have little trouble navigating new websites. Plus, many institutions already have work-study programs in the budget. Faculty send in lists of their current resources, and students compile potential open resource alternatives. Faculty then pick what they want to use from the suggestions. Individual faculty might also employ graduate teaching assistants to search for OER.

Badges

In 2016 Florida International University came up with a badging system to encourage faculty to adopt OER (FIU Online, n.d.). It first established a target of having total educational resources for a course cost no more than $20 per credit. It then invited faculty who met this target to apply for an "affordability counts" medallion that would be awarded to their course and displayed on both the syllabus and learning management system. One would hope that these badges are also displayed in the course catalog and elsewhere outside the course itself; they cannot really motivate students to choose the course if the student needs to already be enrolled to see it.

Fifty-four courses received the medallion in the program's first year; today that number is 150. The program initially targeted online courses, perhaps because these faculty are already attuned to electronic resources, though the hope is to expand it to face-to-face offerings as well. Other institutions that adopt similar programs might find that courses with these badges draw students away from courses without badges, thus incentivizing faculty who teach electives to offer them as well. This could eventually snowball into widespread adoption by faculty around the institution.

Money

Perhaps the most radical and potentially most effective means of gaining faculty buy-in is with financial incentives. The University of Idaho tried just that when it offered grants of up to $2,000 to faculty who adopted OER for their courses (Staben, 2019). But Chuck Staben, the university's president, wants to go even further: to implement a revenue plan whereby the academic department, teaching center, and library would each receive a percentage of students' total textbook savings according to the formula "5 percent/2.5 percent/2.5 percent, respectively."

Given that student savings do not go into the institution's pockets, where would this money come from? Staben suggests that even a small increase in student retention due to the program would be sufficient to pay for it. Plus, a state-supported institution can lobby its legislators to earmark money for OER initiatives on grounds that they save taxpaying students money.

Hopefully, many more institutions will begin implementing OER programs to save students money and increase retention.

References

Feldstein, A., Martin, M., Hudson, A., Warren, K., Hilton, J., III, & Wiley, D. (2012). Open textbooks and increased student access and outcomes. *European Journal of Open, Distance and E-Learning*. Retrieved from http://www.eurodl.org/?p=archives&year=2012&halfyear=2&article=533

FIU Online. (n.d.). *Affordability Counts framework*. Retrieved from https://dlss.flvc.org/documents/210036/1254784/Affordability+Counts+-+FIU.pdf/967c9a4a-d93e-a7b1-24f3-77db6996c7bf

Lieberman, M. (2018, June 20). Trial and error: Students and alumni lead OER factory. *Inside Higher Education*. Retrieved from https://www.insidehighered.com/digital-learning/article/2018/06/20/students-lead-curation-oer-materials-professors-college-canyons

Seaman, J. E., & Seaman, J. (2017). *Opening the textbook: Educational resources in U.S. higher education, 2017*. Retrieved from http://www.onlinelearningsurvey.com/reports/openingthetextbook2017.pdf

Staben, C. (2019, February 13). A new way to motivate faculty adoption of OER. *Inside Higher Education*. Retrieved from https://www.insidehighered.com/digital-learning/views/2019/02/13/encourage-faculty-adoption-oer-share-savings-departments-and

Both Sides Now: Creating a Culture of UDL

Danielle Wilken

In a 1969 song, Joni Mitchell tells us of how she's looked at life from "Both Sides, Now." That is sage advice for considering how Universal Design for Learning (UDL) can benefit students when faculty and administration examine their hopes (and fears) for creating a new learning experience.

At two recent conferences within a single week, I led discussions about adopting UDL as a pedagogical approach for supporting diverse groups of student learners.

At the beginning of the week, I participated in a breakfast conversation for chief academic officers (CAOs) from across the United States. They expressed their frustrations in trying to get faculty and administration to collaboratively support students according to a single shared vision for their academic departments. The CAOs encountered so much faculty resistance that, despite their leadership roles, they felt unable to make the vision a reality.

A few days later, I facilitated a discussion at a UDL in higher education conference at which most participants were instructors from throughout the country. This time I heard that while faculty would like to create a culture of teaching excellence on their campuses, they perceived school leaders as paying lip service to such initiatives and failing to provide the leadership and support needed for such a significant culture change to take place.

So what *is* needed for college administration and faculty to successfully create a culture of UDL in service to their students?

In 2017, Goodwin University in East Hartford, Connecticut, formally adopted UDL as our pedagogical approach to support our students. According to CAST (n.d.), which developed it, UDL is a "framework to improve and optimize teaching and learning for all people based on scientific insights into how humans learn." The framework focuses on three principles of learning: *engagement* (the why), *representation* (the what), and *action and expression* (the how).

The UDL model (CAST, 2011) involves developing curricula, implementing instruction, and assessing learning in a way that gives each student equal access to learning. An underlying assumption of UDL is that students learn best when given a variety of methods and opportunities to access and apply knowledge. Goodwin chose the framework because of its scientific foundation; its recognition in the 2008 Higher Education Opportunity Act, which mentions it 18 times (Roberts et al., 2011); and its inclusive focus, which is consistent with Goodwin's student population.

Our foray into UDL began with a simple declaration: "We are adopting UDL as our institutional pedagogical approach." At an introductory professional development event with Goodwin faculty, I led with a standard UDL strategy: identifying the goal of the learning and being explicit about it.

I laid out a vision for Goodwin's future in which UDL would be a consistent part of how we taught our students, designed curriculum, and created assessments. The purpose of the event was to create a common understanding of both the principles of UDL and our expectations as an institution. I wasn't subtle, and I didn't try to sneak it in as if it were a vitamin that was good for the faculty but that they wouldn't appreciate. I also presented the professional learning model that we would use going forward: sustained, job-embedded, learning community cohorts that would train 15 faculty members at a time.

As anticipated, some faculty members completely embraced the idea, while others were less enthusiastic. The adopters and the resisters, however, did not fall along the expected disciplinary or content lines. Predictably, some English and sociology faculty immediately took to the concept, but there were also psychology faculty who suggested we were lowering the academic bar—creating chaotic classrooms, run by students without any control. There was genuine concern that students would be allowed to turn in any assignment they wished without the faculty being able to hold them to a standard. Additionally, faculty in the STEM and health science disciplines raised the point that because we have strong pass rates in our selective admission programs leading to licensure, we should not tamper with our current teaching methods. But a math faculty member and the director of a selective admission licensure program were among the first individuals to apply for our first cohort of UDL fellows. As I experienced resistance to this initiative, both overt and covert, my standard reply was, "This isn't mandatory. It's *your* choice to participate."

Then the real work began: an eight-session professional learning experience that took place over several months. Cohort 1 consisted of 15 faculty members representing a variety of disciplines as well as a broad range of teaching experience, from a first-time adjunct to a 15-year veteran instructor. The training modeled the principles of UDL and was designed to be sustained, intensive, and job-embedded and provide plentiful opportunities to learn and practice.

The feedback we received from our first cohort was overwhelmingly positive. Cohort 1 enthusiastically influenced the remainder of the faculty, Cohort 2 filled up quickly and included more disciplinary diversity, and we've never looked back. Cohort 3 had 32 applicants for 15 slots. To date, we have trained 43 of our approximately 93 full and 202 part-time faculty members, and our fourth cohort will begin early this year. In addition, in response to requests from staff who recognize the opportunity to use UDL to inform and influence their work with students, we are preparing to launch an inaugural staff cohort in 2020. Perhaps most notably, we launched the Goodwin University Institute for Learning Innovation in November 2019. The institute is a direct result of the work that the university has done with faculty training, and the result of the faculty's commitment to UDL. Equally important, it is a way to highlight the impact on students, including their level of engagement with course materials and faculty.

Achieving this level of success and establishing the institute has resulted from a collaborative, iterative, and ongoing dialogue between the administration and faculty. It began with the first group of faculty and has continued since. Leading up to the conclusion of Cohort 1's training, it became evident that we had created something special that needed to be celebrated and nurtured. The goal of planting deep roots and fostering a culture of UDL was being realized.

The initial incentive to participate in Cohort 1 was a nominal stipend, but it has evolved since their "graduation." The following is a list of benefits associated with participation in a UDL cohort:

- **UDL teaching fellow designation:** Prior to Cohort 1's graduation, the UDL leadership team developed the concept of the UDL teaching fellow, a designation given only to faculty who complete the UDL training. Faculty are noted in the college catalog with this designation and permitted to include it in their profiles and email signatures. Perhaps most importantly and symbolically, fellows are recognized at a college-wide event where they are presented their certificates by the college president.
- **Final presentation lunch with senior college leaders:** When faculty finish their training, we celebrate their accomplishments with a lunch

at their final session, where they present assignments they revised using UDL principles and discuss the impact on their students. Members of senior college leadership always stop by to thank faculty for their commitment to their craft and our students.
- **Teaching fellows classroom fund:** I realized that in some cases faculty were spending their own money on equipment or software to support their UDL-based teaching. As a result I created the UDL Fellows Teaching Fund, to which fellows can apply for stipends to support the work in their classroom.
- **UDL active learning classrooms:** In my discussions with Fellows about challenges they faced as they changed their teaching, they reported that while our regular classrooms are new and beautiful, the traditional seating does not support the active learning strategies that they were employing as a result of their training. They were spending too much time rearranging furniture. Using their feedback, we partnered with Steelcase, a furniture company with a good deal of experience in educational environments, to design four UDL-specific classrooms with active learning furniture, available only for fellows' use.
- **UDL community of practice (CoP) membership:** After completing their training, Cohort 1 refused to disband. They had become a very tight-knit, cohesive group who wanted to continue the conversation and supporting each other. As a result, every semester we now sponsor a CoP event for fellows that may include professional development, conversation, or a state-of-the-union type discussion.

We have made significant progress toward our goal of using UDL as a framework to teach students, design curriculum, and create assessments. While establishing this type of initiative does require a nominal financial investment, it is well worth the return in educational value. More importantly, it takes time, commitment, and trust—the keys to administration and faculty enjoying joint ownership of the initiative. Both sides, now.

References

CAST. (n.d.). About Universal Design for Learning. Retrieved from http://www.cast.org/our-work/about-udl.html#.XelERuhKiUk

CAST. (2011). *Universal Design for Learning Guidelines version 2.0*. Wakefield, MA: CAST.

Roberts, K. D., Park, H. J., Brown, S., & Cook, B. (2011). Universal Design for Instruction in postsecondary education: A systematic review of empirically based articles. *Journal of Postsecondary Education and Disability, 24*(1), 5–15.

Program Acquisitions: Lessons for Leaders

Katie J. Fischer

In my role as dean of the College of Health and Science at Concordia University, St. Paul (CSP), I collaborated in the acquisition of two resource-intensive healthcare programs associated with university closures. In December 2016, CSP began the acquisition process for a pre-licensure nursing program, and, in March 2019, CSP acquired a diagnostic medical sonography program. Currently, in April 2020, CSP is pursuing the acquisition of a third program, a pre-licensure nursing program in another state also associated with a university closure. The acquisitions had similarities and differences, with one primary dissimilarity being my leadership and recognition of lessons learned from previous acquisitions. If you find yourself in a similar position in which you are wondering about program acquisition, here are some suggestions to guide you along your way.

1. Use an acquisition team

Involve key stakeholders in the acquisition process and use existing processes. It is helpful to include human resources, the provost, the chief financial officer, assessment and accreditation, and others as needed. The size of the acquisition will determine the key team members. Based on my experience, open-minded colleagues who view acquisitions as opportunities to support a new group of students and faculty and the university mission make for a strong, impactful team. Trust your colleagues' expertise and the processes in place to guide the decisions needing to be made throughout the acquisition.

2. Review the program(s) for institutional fit, synergy, and shared values

Our institution had already identified the desire to add pre-licensure nursing and diagnostic medical sonography programs via strategic growth in health sciences, but it was not ready to begin development. Acquiring the programs presented a unique opportunity to begin them in a quicker and less expensive, albeit nontraditional, manner. A recommendation is to have a list of future programs the university would consider adding through its own development or acquisition (or both): review programs for institutional fit, synergy with existing programs, and shared values of the institution. This early review will accelerate your institution's ability to move quickly on an acquisition. Once you decide to acquire a program, it is also important to use your existing processes for program review and approval. Accrediting agencies will want to verify existing processes and policies were used.

3. Show care and concern for the students involved

Students are in a vulnerable position when their institution closes. They are looking for answers. It is recommended that one person in the enrollment management or admissions office be the primary contact for student inquiries to ensure that students receive consistent messages. We shared factual information from accreditors (e.g., timeline of program review) with students so they could make informed decisions about their future educational paths.

4. Show care and concern for the faculty involved

My biggest lesson learned is this one: people are everything. Each institution needs to determine whether to hire the faculty in the acquired program(s) (see #7 below). If faculty and staff are brought over with the program, they will be under a great deal of stress and uncertainty. They will wonder, *Will I have a job well into the future? What will happen to my students? What is the culture of the new university? Who will I report to? What will the program look like now that another university is offering it?* It is imperative that you show care and concern for the people involved. Get to know them as people and colleagues. Empathize with them for the loss they are experiencing and the acquisition's impact on students and colleagues at their previous university. I found that throughout CSP's first two acquisitions, my focus changed. It became less about strategy and more about building trust and relationships. In the current acquisition, I am again focusing on the people involved. One note: If you have faculty who have been brought over as part of an acquisition, recognize that any university closures in the news will likely evoke stressful memories. Continue to check in with those colleagues and provide support.

5. Accreditation, accreditation, accreditation

This point is vital: student success is the rationale for the acquisition, and faculty are key to the success of any strategy associated with accreditation. It is important to involve regional accreditors, programmatic accreditors (when applicable), and regulatory agencies early in the acquisition process. Learn the policies and regulations associated with the acquisition and collaborate with agencies to find an optimal resolution. During each of CSP's acquisitions, I have appreciated the accreditation processes as they have ensured the programs' quality—an added reassurance for everyone associated with the programs.

6. Conduct an interview or alternate process for prospective employees

Each institution needs to determine whether the employees in the acquired program(s) will transition to the new institution. An interview or a different screening process can be helpful for both the university and the prospective faculty. It gives the university time to learn about the prospective employees, and it allows prospective faculty to assess the institution's culture and expectations and whether they can envision a future with the school.

7. Find ways to initiate newly hired faculty to your institution's culture

Similar to faculty with experience at previous institution(s), your new faculty may understand how to be faculty at their old institution, but unfortunately that experience does not translate to an understanding of your institution. To succeed at your institution, they need to learn your expectations and culture. Be intentional about the onboarding process. Use seminars, mentorship models, and general conversation to acclimate them to your institution. At CSP, we hosted a semester-long seminar, along with intentional one-on-one and group conversations, to connect faculty to other new hires and help them learn more about the ethos of the institution.

8. Include faculty at your existing institution

Faculty governance is an important part of any institution. At CSP, I am grateful to the many colleagues who supported each acquisition. Faculty have been helpful with vetting acquisition opportunities (we recently said no to one opportunity), pursuing program approvals and associated policy updates, and providing overall guidance regarding implementation. Our faculty continue to focus on student success, and program acquisition has been one way to support a new student audience.

9. Communicate often while also embracing uncertainty

My previous acquisition experience has given me a general sense of the acquisition process, but the mechanics of each acquisition have differed due to the many variables involved. There is much uncertainty associated with acquisitions. My takeaway is to not wait too long to communicate with the various groups: current faculty, prospective employees, and students. Communicate intentionally and remember that all parties will pore over each word on account of the emotions involved. I have found that early and ongoing communication, even if I do not know all the details, helps to build relationships and encourage collaboration.

10. Practice self-care and encourage others to do the same

The acquisition process is stressful and requires a significant time investment. I felt a responsibility to the prospective students and prospective employees to provide a positive next step for each program. While we could not change the circumstances of the closures, we could work diligently to get the program approved and accepting students as soon as possible. The ongoing stressors associated with the acquisitions have led me to recommend that leaders prioritize self-care in the form of healthy eating, exercise, and striving for a full night's sleep. I have found that practicing these self-care activities has made me a stronger leader and more equipped to be a better source of support for others.

Acquisitions provide an exciting opportunity to serve additional students in support of your university's mission. Remember to stick to the process, and, most importantly, focus on people.

About the Contributors

T. Renee Ballard is the employee relations and benefits specialist for the human resources department at the University of Wyoming. She spent several years serving on the UW Staff Senate, culminating recently in a term as its president. She is also a student in the university's MA degree program in higher education administration.

Jeffrey L. Buller, PhD, is the author of more than 20 books on academic leadership as well as over 200 articles, essays, and reviews. Along with Robert E. Cipriano, Buller serves a senior partner in ATLAS: Academic Training, Leadership, & Assessment Services, through which he presents webinars and workshops on academic leadership all over the world.

Timothy R. Bussey, PhD, is the associate director for the Office of Diversity, Equity, and Inclusion at Kenyon College, where they specialize in fostering LGBTQ+ inclusion and equity on campus. Previously, they also served as a visiting assistant professor of women's and gender studies at Kenyon, where they taught the college's first permanent queer studies course. They have nearly a decade of teaching experience—both in-person and online—at major research universities, mid-sized institutions, and smaller liberal arts colleges. Their recent works have been published by *Faculty Focus*, *The Conversation*, *BUST Magazine*, and *The Gay & Lesbian Review*, among others.

Russell Carpenter, PhD, is executive director of the Noel Studio for Academic Creativity and Faculty Center for Teaching & Learning as well as professor of English at Eastern Kentucky University. Carpenter is editor of the *Journal of Faculty Development*.

Edna B. Chun, DM, is an award-winning author and thought leader with more than two decades of experience in higher education. Currently, Chun is chief learning officer with HigherEd Talent, a national HR and diversity consulting firm. Her particular expertise is in the development of concrete, research-based strategies that strengthen organizational synergy and build more inclusive cultures in support of institutional goals. Dr. Chun is currently teaching in the human capital management program in the School of Professional Studies at Columbia University.

Robert E. Cipriano, EdD, is a senior partner in ATLAS, an internally acclaimed consulting firm that specializes in academic leadership training and collegiality assessment. He has written extensively on the topics of civility and collegiality, managing conflict, and chairs' perceptions. He served as a department chair for 28 years and received his doctorate in therapeutic recreation with a cognate specialization area of college teaching from New York University.

Jon Crylen, PhD, is editor of online publications for Magna Publications. He received his doctorate in film studies from the University of Iowa (UI) and has taught film courses at both UI and Coe College. His writing, which focuses on environmental film and media, has appeared in the *Journal of Cinema and Media Studies*, *Media Fields Journal*, and *In Media Res* and is forthcoming in *A Cultural History of the Sea in the Global Age* (Bloomsbury) and *Cinema of Exploration: Essays on an Adventurous Film Practice* (Routledge).

Stephanie Delaney, PhD, is the vice president of instruction at Renton Technical College. Delaney has a strong background in guided pathways and e-learning, and she has spoken nationally on issues related to leadership, technology, and effective online teaching and learning.

Kevin Dvorak, PhD, is executive director of the Writing and Communication Center at Nova Southeastern University, where he is also a professor and faculty coordinator for first-year experience. Dvorak is associate editor of the *Journal of Faculty Development*.

Alvin Evans, MEd, is an award-winning author with more than two decades of experience in higher education. Currently, Evans is higher education practice leader with HigherEd Talent, a national HR and diversity consulting firm.

Katie Fischer, DrPH, serves as the dean of the College of Health and Science at Concordia University, St. Paul. Since joining the faculty in 2010, she has developed and taught in-class and online courses related to public health, exercise science, and health care administration. Fischer's background in higher education includes administration of in-class and online programs, collaborative programming, and development of new programs, including the acquisition of three resource-intensive programs from closing institutions.

Timothy Forde, PhD, is vice provost of diversity and associate professor in the College of Education at Eastern Kentucky University. Forde is associate editor for diversity and inclusive excellence of the *Journal of Faculty Development*.

Jon M. Garon, JD, is dean of Nova Southeastern University Shepard Broad College of Law. He is a nationally recognized authority who teaches and writes on technology law, intellectual property, copyright, entertainment, and information privacy. He has written four books along with numerous book chapters and articles. He earned his BA from the University of Minnesota and his JD from Columbia University School of Law.

Eden Gillott Bowe is president of a strategic communications firm, Gillott Communications, and is a former business professor. Bowe has appeared in the *Los Angeles Times*, the *Wall Street Journal*, NPR, the *Washington Post*, *Forbes*, *Financial Times*, *Attorney at Law Magazine*, and *Business Rockstars*. She has authored *A Board Member's Guide to Crisis PR* and *A Lawyer's Guide to Crisis PR*.

Marissa Greenberg, PhD, is an associate professor of English at the University of New Mexico. She has 20 years of experience teaching in-person, hybrid, and fully online classes and participates regularly in faculty course development for the Center for Digital Learning.

Lindsay N. Heinzman is executive director of development and alumni affairs in the School of Science at Indiana University–Purdue University Indianapolis.

Stephanie Hinshaw, MBA, is the senior vice president of academic affairs at American College of Education (ACE). Hinshaw holds a BA in journalism from Indiana University and an MBA in marketing from Butler University. At present, Hinshaw is pursuing a doctorate of education in interdisciplinary leadership at Creighton University anticipated to complete in fall 2020. Her dissertation research centers around the impacts of toxic leaders on their followers.

Lauren A. Kay-Beason is executive director of marketing and media relations in the School of Science at Indiana University–Purdue University Indianapolis.

Masha Krsmanovic, PhD, is an assistant professor of higher education at the University of Southern Mississippi. Krsmanovic is book review editor of the *Journal of Faculty Development*.

N. Douglas Lees, PhD, most recently served as associate dean for planning and finance in the School of Science at Indiana University–Purdue University Indianapolis. His scholarly interests have been directed at higher education change and how that impacts the work of department and school leadership. He is the author of the book *Chairing Academic Departments: Traditional and Emerging Expectations*, Bolton, MA, Anker Publishing (now held by Jossey-Bass), 2006.

Elizabeth "Beth" Lewis is an English instructor at Wake Technical Community College. Beth believes civil discourse is essential to an effective, productive work environment and actively co-leads Wake Tech's Campus Civility Project. To encourage student engagement and thoughtful discussion on campus, Beth created an annual visiting lecture series/speaker event at Wake Tech.

Vance S. Martin, PhD, is the campus accessibility specialist at the University of Illinois Springfield and disability resource advisor for the University of Illinois Board of Trustees. For over 15 years he has taught undergraduate and graduate courses in history, humanities, education and technology using in-person, online, and hybrid formats. He has over 10 years of experience working with accessibility, instructional design, and curriculum design.

Thomas R. McDaniel, PhD, is professor emeritus of education at Converse College. Over his 50-year tenure, he has been a dean as well as provost, interim president, and senior vice president. He holds MAT, MLA, and PhD degrees from Johns Hopkins University. Author of nine books, 35 textbook chapters, and 300 professional journal articles, he is a consulting editor for Academic Leader and an executive editor of *The Clearing House*, a journal for secondary educators.

Emily Moore, MEd, BA, is the department head of the communication and theatre department at Wake Technical Community College. Moore currently represents all college department heads and directors on Wake Tech's Collaborative Council. In this role, she works with other college leaders to resolve conflicts, share information, and make decisions designed to improve the institutional culture and climate of the college.

John Orlando, PhD, serves as the associate director of the Faculty Resource Center at Northcentral University. He edits the Online Cl@ssroom portion of *The Teaching Professor* newsletter. Orlando has published over 75 articles and delivered over 50 presentations, workshops, and keynotes on online education, teaching with technology, and social media. He is a passionate education consultant, educator, and educational administrator helping teachers learn how to use technology to transform their teaching practice and improve student performance.

W. Reed Scull, EdD, is an associate professor in the higher education administration program at the University of Wyoming. He has served in administrative capacities at the University of Nevada, Reno, and the University of Wyoming.

Abdelilah Salim Sehlaoui, EdD, is a professor of TESOL and applied linguistics, currently serving as College of Education Director of Grant Research at Sam Houston State University. He has more than 33 years combined experience in leadership as an educator, teacher educator, and administrator and has knowledge of effective, scientifically proven instructional strategies. He is currently CAEP National Site Reviewer and has wide experience with educational technology and online learning since 2000.

Michael G. Strawser, PhD, is assistant professor of communication at the University of Central Florida. Strawser is managing editor of the *Journal of Faculty Development*.

Tanjula Petty, EdD, currently serves as the assistant provost of academic affairs for Alabama State University. Dr. Petty received a BS in resource management and MS in public administration from Troy State University. She completed her doctoral studies at Alabama State University in educational leadership, policy, and law.

Simon J. Rhodes, PhD, is provost and vice president for academic affairs at the University of North Florida and former dean of the School of Science at Indiana University–Purdue University Indianapolis. Dr. Simon Rhodes received a PhD in biochemistry/biological sciences from Purdue

University, West Lafayette, Indiana.

Brian Udermann, PhD, started teaching online in 2005 and served as the director of online education at the University of Wisconsin–La Crosse from 2007 to 2020. He is a professor in the Department of Exercise and Sport Science at the University. Udermann has written two books, five book chapters, and has published over 70 manuscripts in peer-reviewed journals. He has also given over 200 presentations at state, national, and international meetings and conferences.

Danielle S. Wilken, EdD, MT(ASCP), is provost and dean of faculty at Goodwin University. Wilken has more than 20 years' experience in higher education and has extensive experience in new program and curriculum development, including the launching of a number of degrees at Goodwin. Additionally, she champions the Universal Design for Learning teaching initiative on campus.

Elizabeth Williamson, PhD, is the dean of faculty hiring and development at The Evergreen State College. She oversees new faculty training, ongoing professional development for all faculty members, and workshops on developing inclusive and accessible online courses. She has 20 years of teaching experience, focusing on interdisciplinary, student-centered learning.

Additional Resources
from Magna Publications

BULK PURCHASES

To purchase multiple print copies of this book, please contact Magna Sales at sales@magnapubs.com or call 800-433-0499 ext. 183.

MEMBERSHIPS/SUBSCRIPTIONS

Faculty Focus
www.facultyfocus.com
A free e-newsletter on effective teaching strategies for the college classroom.

Academic Leader Membership
www.Academic-Leader.com
Academic Leader covers the trends, challenges, and best practices today's academic decision-makers. Members gain access to the latest thinking in academic leadership and learn how peers at other institutions are solving problems, managing change, and setting direction. New articles are published throughout the month.

The Teaching Professor Membership
www.TeachingProfessor.com
The Teaching Professor is an annual membership that reflects the changing needs of today's college faculty and the students they teach. This fully online version of the newsletter that faculty have enjoyed for more than 30 years includes the best of the print version—great articles and practical, evidence-based insights—but also many new features including video, graphics, and links that make it an even more indispensable resource.

CONFERENCES

Leadership in Higher Education Conference
www.AcademicLeadershipConference.com
The Leadership in Higher Education Conference provides higher-education leaders with an opportunity to expand leadership skills with proactive strategies, engaging networking, time-saving tips, and best practices.

The Teaching Professor Annual Conference
www.TeachingProfessorConference.com
This event provides an opportunity to learn effective pedagogical techniques, hear from leading teaching experts, and interact with colleagues committed to teaching and learning excellence. Join more than 1,000 educators from around the country.

Attendees hear from a roster of prestigious experts and nationally recognized thought leaders. A broad mix of plenary addresses, concurrent sessions, and timely roundtable discussions leave no topic untouched.

BOOKS

The Academic Leader's Handbook: A Resource Collection for College Administrators
https://www.amazon.com/dp/B0764KMC5Z
The Academic Leader's Handbook: A Resource Collection for College Administrators details an array of proven management strategies and will help further your achievements as a leader in higher education. Discover new leadership tools and insights at departmental, administrative, and executive levels.

Active Learning: A Practical Guide for College Faculty
https://www.amazon.com/dp/B071ZN8R32
Learn how to apply active learning methods in both small and large classes as well as in an online teaching environment. Whether you are new to active learning methods or experienced with them, this comprehensive reference book can guide you every step of the way.

The College Teacher's Handbook: A Resource Collection for New Faculty
https://www.amazon.com/dp/0912150688
The College Teacher's Handbook: A Resource Collection for New Faculty provides the essential tools and information that any new teacher in higher education needs to confidently lead a college classroom.

Essential Teaching Principles: A Resource Collection for Adjunct Faculty
https://www.amazon.com/dp/0912150246
This book provides a wealth of both research-driven and classroom-tested best practices to help adjuncts develop the knowledge and skills required to run a successful classroom. Compact and reader-friendly, this book is conveniently organized to serve as a ready reference whenever a new teaching challenge arises—whether it's refreshing older course design, overcoming a student's objection to a grade, or fine-tuning assessments.

Essential Teaching Principles: A Resource Collection for Teachers
https://www.amazon.com/dp/0912150580
This book serves as a quick and ready reference as you encounter the challenges of teaching college-level material in the high school classroom. For an AP or IB teacher, there's no better resource.

Faculty Development: A Resource Collection for Academic Leaders
https://www.amazon.com/dp/0912150661
Discover proven tips and insights, from top academic experts, that will help you enhance faculty development programming and training on your campus.

Flipping the College Classroom: Practical Advice from Faculty
https://www.amazon.com/dp/B01N2GZ61O
This collection is a comprehensive guide to flipping no matter how much—or how little—experience you have with it. If you are just getting started, you will learn where and how to begin. If you have been at it for a while, you will find new ideas to try and solutions to common challenges. Flipping the College Classroom: Practical Advice from Faculty is an invaluable resource that covers all the necessary territory.

Grading Strategies for the Online College Classroom: A Collection of Articles for Faculty
https://www.amazon.com/dp/0912150564
Do your grading practices accurately reflect your online students' performance? Do your assessment and feedback methods inspire learning? Are you managing the time you spend on these things—or is the workload overwhelming? Grading Strategies for the Online College Classroom: A Collection of Articles for Faculty can help you master the techniques of effective online grading—while avoiding some of the more costly pitfalls.

Helping Students Learn: Resources, Tools, and Activities for College Educators
https://www.amazon.com/dp/0912150602
This workbook is a must-have guide for faculty. While the roles in the college classroom often are defined by teachers teaching and students learning, the reality is that not many students have a clear understanding of how to learn.

Managing Adjunct Faculty: A Resource Collection for Administrators
https://www.amazon.com/dp/B01N2OVK5W
Chances are your adjunct population has been built on an ad hoc basis to fill instructional needs. As a result, your institution might not have a solid management framework to support them. That's a gap you can close with guidance from Managing Adjunct Faculty: A Resource Collection for Administrators. This invaluable guide offers an extensive review of best practices for managing an adjunct cohort and integrating them more fully into your campus community.

The New Dean's Survival Guide: Advice from an Academic Leader
https://www.amazon.com/dp/091215070X
Have you been newly hired as a dean or are you looking for practical tips to help you navigate the challenges and responsibilities in your position as an academic leader? Find numerous tools and strategies to address challenges, successes, and issues leaders face with this comprehensive survival guide with advice for deans, provosts, and managers in higher education.

Planning and Designing Your College Course
https://www.amazon.com/dp/0912150742
Planning and Designing Your College Course focuses on the planning aspects that precede the launching of a course—the work instructors do behind the scenes and that students usually aren't privy to. You'll be able to make each key part of your course design learner-centered and obtain strategies to get students to collaborate in the course design process.

Teaching Strategies for the Online College Classroom: A Collection of Articles for Faculty
https://www.amazon.com/dp/0912150483
Includes online teaching strategies ranging from building a successful start of the semester, fostering productive connections, managing challenging behavior in the online classroom, and enhancing student engagement.

As a special thank you

for purchasing *Leading through Crisis, Conflict, and Change in Higher Education*, we've added three articles that you won't want to miss.

Bonus Content:

Recruiting Subject Matter Experts for Curriculum and Course Design: Three Nonmonetary Strategies
By Becky Costello, EdD

Promoting Faculty Development on a Tight Budget
By Jodie N. Mader, PhD

Fundraising for Academic Leaders: Five Practical Strategies for Deans and Department Chairs
By Craig Hlavac, EdD

Sign up at
www.magnapubs.com/leading-through-crisis

www.ingramcontent.com/pod-product-compliance
Lightning Source LLC
Chambersburg PA
CBHW070807230426
43665CB00017B/2525